Executive Writing Skills for Managers

Better
Business
English

Executive Writing Skills for Managers

Master word power to lead your teams, make strategic links and develop relationships

Fiona Talbot

**KOGAN
PAGE**

London and Philadelphia

Publisher's note

Every possible effort has been made to ensure that the information contained in this book is accurate at the time of going to press, and the publishers and author cannot accept responsibility for any errors or omissions, however caused. No responsibility for loss or damage occasioned to any person acting, or refraining from action, as a result of the material in this publication can be accepted by the editor, the publisher or the author.

First published in Great Britain and the United States in 2009 by Kogan Page Limited

120 Pentonville Road
London N1 9JN
United Kingdom
www.koganpage.com

525 South 4th Street, #241
Philadelphia PA 19147
USA

© Fiona Talbot, 2009

ISBN 978 0 7494 5518 7

British Library Cataloguing-in-Publication Data

A CIP record for this book is available from the British Library.

Library of Congress Cataloging-in-Publication Data

Talbot, Fiona.
  Executive writing skills for managers : master word power to lead your teams, make strategic links, and develop relationships / Fiona Talbot.
      p. cm.
  Includes bibliographical references.
  ISBN 978-0-7494-5518-7
  1. Business writing. 2. English language--Business English. 3. Commercial correspondence. I. Title.
  HF5718.3.T35 2009
  658.4'53--dc22

                                                                2009016005

Typeset by JS Typesetting Ltd, Porthcawl, Mid Glamorgan
Printed and bound in India by Replika Press Pvt Ltd

Dedication

I would like to thank my family, friends and clients for their support throughout my career. It is a wonderful fact that, by sharing experiences and lessons learnt, we all learn from each other, to our mutual benefit.

Special thanks must go to my dear husband, Colin. I would like to dedicate this series to him – and to my son, Alexander, and my daughter, Hannah-Maria. And to my mother, Lima.

Contents

Preface

How this series works – and what it is about

There are three books in the series, designed to improve your confidence and competence in writing English for global business. They are designed on three levels, to fit in with the three stages in the business cycle.

My central philosophy is this: writing business English effectively for international trade is about creating clear, concise messages and avoiding verbosity. But the fewer words you write, the more important it is that you get them right.

Book 1: How to Write Effective Business English

This book assumes that you know English to intermediate level and provides effective guidelines. It deals with real-life scenarios, to give you answers that even your boss may not know.

It uses a system that also gives you the building blocks to take you to the next level in the cycle of success, set out in Book 2.

Book 2: Make an Impact with your Written English

This book will take you a further step forward in your executive career.

You will learn how to use written word power to promote and sell your messages, as well as 'brand you'. You will learn how to make your mark writing English, whether for PR, presentations, reports, meeting notes, manuals etc. And for cyberspace, where English is today's predominant language.

You will learn how to deal with pressing challenges that you need to be aware of. And how to write English that impresses, so that you get noticed for the right reasons.

Book 3: Executive Writing Skills for Managers

This book deals with the English business writing you need at the top of your career and focuses on writing as a key business tool.

It gives amazingly valuable tips on harmonizing the English that you and your teams use (for example, for evaluation performance) – tips that you quite simply have not seen before. It also introduces the concept of Word Power Skills 2.0 – for unified English business writing that keeps everyone in the loop.

The importance of business English today

Increasingly, English is the language of choice used in multinational gatherings. It may not be the predominant language of the group, but it is the most likely to be understood by the majority – at least at basic level – so becomes a powerful tool for communication and inclusion.

You may have to unlearn some things you learnt at school

Writing English for business today is highly unlikely to be the same as the writing you were taught at school or university. Apart from getting your punctuation and grammar right, the similarities often end there.

This series works with the business cycle

The series highlights the essential role business writing plays at every stage in your career path – and alongside the cycle of business in general. Figures 1 and 2 show how this works. I describe below how it relates to the three phases.

Phase one: joining an organization or setting up your own business

English business writing needs at the outset of your career: a CV, letter, job application, start-up plan or business plan, routine business writing tasks.

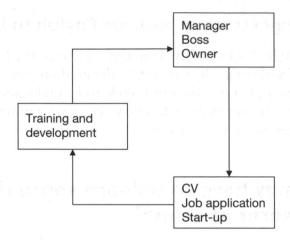

Figure 1 The business cycle: from the individual's perspective

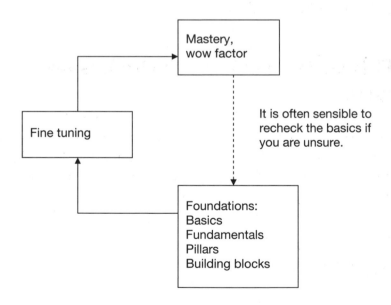

Figure 2 The business cycle: from the business writing perspective

As you start your career, you need to understand how to get the basics right. You need to understand how to write correctly, how spelling, punctuation and grammar matter. You will not get to the next phase in your career – the pitching phase – without getting the basics right.

Phase two: you develop through knowing how to harness word power

Your developing English business writing needs; making impact in everything you write in English; personal self-development or other training.

Great business English writing will generate ideas and sparks that capture readers' attention and take your career forward. Powerful writing can sell your proposals so well – weak writing can do the exact opposite.

Phase three: mastery of written word power enables you to shine and lead

English business writing needs at the height of your career: mastery of written word power required for leadership, to shine as a manager, boss and/or owner.

You do not get to the top by blending in. You have to build bridges, shape outcomes and lead through word power. You need to express your ideas in writing – so use business English that makes readers want to buy in.

The series is an easy, indispensable, comprehensive guide

It is an essential tool kit to keep by your desk or take on your travels. Dip in and out of it as and when you need the answers it provides, to help you shine in all stages of your career.

So each of the three books aligns with the business cycle and supports your development and perfection of writing English for business to gain the competitive edge – because the development of the written word goes hand in hand with, or even is, the business cycle itself.

Get results!

Just take a look at my methods, focus on the elements that apply to your business writing and make sure they become an intrinsic part of your real-life performance.

This series does not take you away from your job; it focuses on your job and uses word power as a free resource. All you have to do is harness this – and enjoy the benefits of immediate results and sustainable improvements.

Good luck on your journey to success!

Fiona Talbot
TQI Word Power Skills
www.wordpowerskills.com

Introduction

By the end of this book you will know how to write business English to take you to the absolute forefront of global business. You will understand how simply expressed facts are the best understood, even where the most complex subject matter is involved.

You are probably conversant with the concept of Web 2.0, in which the web is an interactive, two-way process. This book develops the concept of written Word Power Skills 2.0 to show that actually, interaction is essential in all your written business communication. You will write English that engages buy-in and keeps everyone in the loop.

I

English as a language of global communication

Defining readers, customers and audience

Throughout this book I use the terms readers, target readership, customers and audience interchangeably. I use 'customer' both in its most common usage as a person who buys goods or services from a business, and in the broadest sense of signifying a person that you deal with in the course of your daily work. So the term applies just as much to internal colleagues, suppliers, those in the public sector etc as it does to those who are external buying consumers.

Your audience can be anyone and everyone

I use many practical examples and scenarios in this book that relate to standard sales or customer pitches. Because we are all consumers in our private lives, we can easily relate to and understand these examples. What I would like to stress is that the concepts apply equally to every scenario in the list that follows. Think of lobbying; think of politics; think of charities; think of fundraising; think of promotions.

Cross-cultural differences in writing

Agree on the business English to use in your sector

Before considering how to deal with any cross-cultural differences in writing, it is a good idea to define what you mean by business English. This may be for:

- communicating within your organization;
- communicating with external readers generally;
- communicating with a particular sector.

You see, there can be far-reaching consequences if you unknowingly mix modes.

Let me explain what I mean by business English. As we know, English is a major language of commercial communication generally. It is also the world's language of the internet and global access to knowledge. Business English is quite simply the name given to the English used for dealing with business communication in English. Defining English itself is more complicated, however, as there are many varieties.

I use a 'standard UK English' throughout this book that is likely to be understood in international business. It is the English you see in most mainstream UK English dictionaries and grammar books – though it may not be used in a standard way by differing cultures. So this book is about helping you design English writing that works for most readers.

When I write in this book about 'native English speakers', I mean anyone who speaks any variety of English as their first language. Non-native English speakers may learn English in any of the following categories: English as an acquired language (EAL), English as a foreign language (EFL) and English for speakers of other languages (ESOL), which are self-explanatory terms; and English as a second language (ESL). In the ESL category, learners are likely to be in a setting where the main or official language is English but their native tongue is not. It can be a confusing term when used to describe someone who is actually learning English as a third or fourth language, as can be the case.

There is some debate within academic circles as to which of these terms (or others) should be used. As this is not an academic but a business-oriented book, I choose to use a different convention here. Throughout the book you will find that I use:

- the term native English (NE) speaker or writer to denote a person whose first language is English, and native English (NE) writing to refer to their writing;

- the term non-native English (non-NE) speaker or writer to denote a person whose first language is not English, and non-native English (non-NE) writing to refer to their writing.

Without a doubt, the way English can be written in business can puzzle both NE and non-NE speakers alike. Sometimes it is because non-NE writers use it in unusual ways. One example that springs to mind is the continental-European use of the word 'handy' to mean 'mobile phone' in UK English or 'cellphone' in US English.

At other times, written English can puzzle readers because of the different varieties of English. Alongside UK English, you will find US English, Australian English, Caribbean English, Indian English, Singapore English and South African English, to name just some.

Then we find instances such as Chinglish (Chinese-English), Manglish (Malaysian-English) and Singlish (Singapore-English), where English is mixed with some of the language patterns of the native country. Users of Chinglish, to take just one example, may understand perfectly what they mean. But they may still fall into the trap of mistranslating (even to the point of unintelligibility) for the foreign reader. Naturally enough, these mistranslations appear where foreigners are most likely to see them. This can be in public places, on menus in restaurants, on road signs etc, and also where exports are concerned, for example, on product labels or in instructions.

Indeed, during the planning stage for the 2008 Beijing Olympics, the Chinese authorities rightly anticipated a huge influx of foreign visitors. They identified a need to try to root out some of the problems they knew existed. One municipal spokesman voiced their concern, acknowledging that 'this misinformation has become a headache for foreigners'. Examples of the Chinglish the authorities identified were:

'To take notice of safe, the slippery are very crafty' = Warning: slippery path.

In a gym: 'The treadmill is in the middle of repairing' = The treadmill is being repaired.

More non-native speakers of English than native ones

The Chinese are not alone in trying to solve this tricky problem. Did you know that more non-native speakers of English use English than native speakers do?

The UK government currently estimates that more than a billion people speak English, and projections indicate that by 2020 two billion people worldwide will be learning or teaching English. So English is not just for the nation that gives the language its name. It does not belong to a single culture but acts as a bridge across borders and cultures. Whichever variety you choose to use, make sure that it is understood by those with whom you are doing business.

You know how important effective business writing is. Get it right and a company can build on success. Get it wrong and it can contribute to an organization's failure. Why? Because written words are judged for what they are, when we may not be there to explain them. And it can be difficult enough to get them right first time, even in our native language, let alone a foreign one!

Office guidelines and house style can help

If you are leading cross-cultural teams and you want to manage effectively, be one step ahead. Be aware that each member of the team may approach their writing differently. But it's not enough simply to note the differences.

Make a difference

You will be a far more effective manager if you draw up guidelines:

■   to foster some consistency in corporate approach;

■   to help develop effective working relationships in your cross-cultural teams;

■   to then consider making these part of any induction programme that your company may operate.

How? Well, I will show you a four-step guide to premier business writing in Chapter 3, which will outline how to go about it. By the end of the book, you should see a way forward to customizing the tips into guidelines that are right for your business.

Part of the reason that every culture may start from a slightly (or even very) different perspective is this. Much depends on national teaching curricula. Also, teachers may even teach English (or at least some aspects of it) wrongly – in this case it can become hard for learners to break bad habits. Even if not taught wrongly, some nationalities are taught rather old-fashioned styles of English that do not suit today's business writing.

Three practical examples are these. Some teachers still state:

■   that passives are always a better writing style than actives;

■   that you cannot use personal pronouns such as 'I' or 'we' in business writing;

■   that you can never start a sentence in English with 'And' or 'But'.

But actually you can do all of these things – this sentence is an example of one of them. And native English writers do. Pick up any quality business publication in English and you will find these usages over and over again. If, however, you or your company prefer to observe the rules above, including not starting a sentence with 'And' or 'But', then that is a different matter. That's your choice.

Itemize all aspects of what you need to write in English

If you adopt guidelines, be systematic. Itemize all aspects of your writing, so that staff know how to apply house style in each case. Sometimes companies call me in to help as a troubleshooter for specific writing tasks such as report- or minute-writing skills, or letters or marketing material. It is often only later, once I am hired, that they realize that they should not be looking at each task in isolation. Corporate communication has to be joined up. When it is, companies, readers and customers can reap the benefits, such as:

- seeing a consistent, quality professional image;
- appreciating seamless communication rather than the disjointed writing that is the norm for many companies;
- removing from the equation the often all-too-apparent divisiveness (even open competition) that can exist between departments.

Take this opportunity now to write down your business English writing topics. Then you can see at a glance where guidelines are needed.

Your writing should lead by example

If you have a house writing style, make sure you publicize it and that everybody knows where the style guide can be found. And that it is there to be used for each writing task.

Remember that you have to stick to the code too! Staff buy in better when managers practise what they preach. They can inspect managers' writing and look for evidence of best practice. They are open to be persuaded, as if they are saying, 'Show me the best way before I follow!'

A checklist of things to consider

Physical aspects such as font, point size and layout, punctuation, when to use capital letters, date and time conventions etc.

Conveying openness and honesty.

Conveying other company values too.

Selling company messages.

Writing that is results focused and sent at the right time to the right people.

Writing styles that are concise – but not at the cost of not saying the right things.

Tone that is appropriate for the target sector.

The items in the box are not a final list – but you will by now be getting the idea of the type of things that can be involved. However, your work doesn't stop here. Further tips to help you:

■ Don't stop at defining house style and printing guides in hard copy.

■ Post these on the intranet if appropriate.

■ Update them regularly, as business moves on.

■ Cascade any changes through the organization.

Designate a style champion to promote effective writing in English

Designate someone to promote style guidelines if you cannot do this yourself. Get your English right every time. Companies routinely designate champions to promote individual initiatives. Why act differently about the key skill of written communication? There's virtually no cost involved in harnessing written word power effectively. But it will save you money through improved performance.

The four-way mirror approach

Case study

A major Anglo-Dutch company that trades globally through the medium of English was dedicated to achieving cross-cultural business success. Yet it had a problem that was holding it back. Even though only two nationalities – English and Dutch – predominantly made up the workforce, they were often puzzled (and very often exasperated) by their differing approaches and usage in business English writing.

The managing director asked me to suggest a solution. I devised a model that uses a figurative or make-believe mirror approach. It is so easy to grasp and so easy to master that the company told me that in their subsequent Investors in People training assessment, this training was at the forefront of employees' minds. Not only had it helped each nationality understand the other's use of English ('Oh, that's why they write English like that!'), it also helped them understand other cultures' writing perspectives.

This is how the model works. Do try it for yourself.

Imagine you have a mirror in your hand. Hold it up in front of you while you focus on readers as customers, and then answer the following questions:

1.   How do your customers see themselves?

2.   How do you see yourself?

3.   How do you see your customers?

4.   How do your customers see you through your writing?

This approach will help you see how different cultures communicate differently. Even though they may all be using English, their natural tendency will be to use it their way.

Let me outline some broad differences:

- Some cultures choose informality over formality.

- Others do the reverse.

- Some believe that brevity is a virtue.

- Others believe that to get to the point too quickly is actually impolite.

- Some believe in spelling things out.

- Some believe in simply implying something.

- Some believe in the power of the individual.

- Some believe that consensus within the group rules the day.

Now, to go back to the four-way mirror approach, please take this opportunity of answering the four questions I posed above. Let me guide you by giving some ideas from generic observations I have made in the past. You will see the sort of answers companies give.

1. How do your customers see themselves?

Answers often include:

- professional;
- structured, formal;
- focused on the long term;
- team workers;
- polite;
- right.

2. How do you see yourself?

Answers often include:

- professional;
- informal;
- lateral thinking and creative;
- everyone can have their say;
- direct;
- responsive and speedy.

3. How do you see your customers?

Answers often include:

- difficult to understand;
- do not have a rapport with foreigners;
- bureaucratic and inflexible;
- overly polite and hiding behind language;
- slow;
- paying absolute attention to detail.

4. How your customers may see you

Answers often include a mixture of all the points so far made!

When you get your business writing to align with the correct focus for your purpose, your company and your customers, this is when you know you are getting it right.

This exercise is actually great fun to do. It reveals a lot (in quite a light-hearted yet highly meaningful way) about both readers and writers in cross-cultural business environments. Do try it and you will see how easily and well it works.

Writing for exporting

Companies that export sometimes enter this arena quickly – and go for a quick fix. It rarely works to their ultimate advantage, as successful exporting involves more than simply having products and services that are suitable for the export sector. Success can depend just as much on developing good working relationships and being prepared to make a commitment to this on an ongoing basis. That is why the system I show in this book will prove invaluable. It is set out in Chapter 3 and you may find it particularly useful to focus on Step 4. It is about writing to build the right (and sustainable) connections with your readers, as both internal or external customers. It is a manifestation of customer care. And any manager who does not know how to express customer care in writing is likely to come unstuck sooner rather than later.

Incoterms

You may know of abbreviations (acronyms) such as 'ETA' for 'estimated time of arrival' or 'COB' for 'close of business'. There is actually a whole host of such terms, known as inco-terms. These are commonly used trade terms written and abbreviated in English for international trade.

They were devised by the International Chamber of Commerce (ICC) in 1936 (and have been regularly updated since then) because parties to a contract did not always realize that the terms and abbreviations they used could have different implications in different countries. Imagine the problems if the so-called 'standard terms' you are using do not mean the same as those used by the people with whom you are trading. There could be financial and operational implications – and even litigation. If incoterms are likely to be useful to you, you may care to visit the ICC website. The terms can be subject to copyright, so you need to enquire about their use.

For more on acronyms see Chapter 6.

Pitfalls of translating

It can be amazingly difficult for your readers (both native and non-native English speakers) to have to 'translate translated English'. It does not make financial sense, as work is being duplicated. But on the other hand, pretending that broken English is acceptable is not going to be the answer either. It may not actually make sense or it may be misunderstood, as we saw from the Chinglish examples earlier.

So to succeed in writing business English:

■ Express the gist of what you are saying in really accessible English.

■ Do not focus on just translating from your own language into English.

■ Regularly ask yourself questions such as: Will my readers recognize the words I use? Will they understand their meaning? Am I enabling the response I need? Will my business achieve its desired goals as a result?

One-upmanship

'Out-Englishing' the others

Non-NE writers can try to 'out-English' the rest of the field by resolutely using English idioms and puns at every possible opportunity, which can give rise to many problems in business. These problems are largely because:

■ Idioms are, by definition, expressions that are peculiar to a language and can slip in and out of use.

■ Some are more obscure than others, at times even having to be explained to native speakers.

■ Non-NE and sometimes even NE writers can get them wrong.

Examples of wrong usage are:

- 'I feel like a prawn in the game.' This idiom is a chess analogy, so the expression should be 'pawn in the game'. If somebody feels like a pawn in the game, they feel of little value; they are there for someone else's advancement, not their own. Just by wrongly inserting one letter, we get the word 'prawn' (a large shrimp), so the idiom becomes unintentionally comic.

- 'You really helped us to face up even some difficult moment during the project.' The writer has been overambitious here. They wanted to use the English idiom 'face up to difficulties'. They should have said, 'You really helped us face up to some difficulties during the project.' This would mean 'You really helped us confront (or admit) to some difficulties.' The trouble is, the writer got the expression wrong. Far from impressing, they managed to 'out-English' the English. You may make some sense of it but you have to work out the likely meaning. In short, it sounds like English but it is not. And it does not work.

Some examples of English idioms are:

- 'It's raining cats and dogs.' This means 'It's raining heavily.'
- 'Bob's your uncle.' This means 'It's as easy as that.'
- 'The meeting went on till the cows came home.' This means 'The meeting seemed interminable.'

Even correct usage of English idiomatic expressions is still likely to confuse non-NE readers. So I suggest that you avoid them where possible.

'Over-Englishing': the reactions you can produce

I use the term 'over-Englishing' to mean the next level up (or down, depending on your viewpoint!) from 'out-Englishing'. 'Over-Englishing' refers to the desire of some non-native English writers to outdo native English writers with an embellished, exaggerated use of language that deviates from the original. It is all too often an imaginary language, and in the ultimate analysis often has no meaning.

What type of writer 'over-Englishes'? Often they are non-NE writers with self-esteem that is perhaps too high. Confident that they have all the answers, they may feel superior to lesser mortals, as the following gems of 'over-Englishing' show. In both instances, we find two real-life, non-NE job-seekers showcasing their talent – or at least that is what they think they are doing:

- An accountant: 'I dispose of untouchable integrity and corresponding success and my brilliance is impressive.'

- A marketing manager: 'My knowledge, ratio and outstanding attributions decide that my future will be with your company.'

The problem is that this writing is likely to have the opposite effect to that which the writers intended. It is not real English and the claims are pretentious, so neither piece of writing impresses.

Puns

Puns are often used in English – especially in advertising – as jokes that exploit the different meanings of a word.

Case study

An English pun in advertising

An example of a pun in business English is the slogan 'Purr-fection for Jaguar', which appeared in an advertisement for Jaguar cars some years ago.

The pretend English word 'purr-fection' uses a play on the word 'purr'. This can be used in English to signify both the sound of a car engine that is performing well and the sound a cat makes when happy (a jaguar is a member of the cat family).

On another level, the pun also depends on readers understanding that 'purr-fection' makes a parallel play on the word 'perfection'. So the slogan works on a number of levels – for the native English-speaking market, that is.

When you write for global markets, you have to understand that a pun that may be very obvious to you, particularly if you have a sophisticated grasp of English, may not work universally. You need to research whether your audience is likely to understand – and also appreciate – this form of writing. Some do and some do not: it is as simple as that.

Your checklist for action

- See writing as a fundamental skill for you as an individual, and for your business.

- Develop and improve your business English writing at every opportunity throughout your career.

- Remember that business English writing – in its many forms – is your most common route to international markets. Be the best.

- Think about your house style and how you want to come across.

- Understand the four-way mirror approach: there may be differences between how you see yourself and how your cross-cultural customers see you.

- Identify the correct focus, and write to reflect this.

- Do not feel the need to 'out-English' NE writers.

- In business writing, less is often more (though not at the expense of rapport or effective cross-cultural working relationships).

- Understand how wrong translations can give rise to misinformation: a headache for non-native English and native English writers alike.

- English idioms and puns can be difficult to use or understand in international business – so you may need to avoid them.

2

Writing in English: support your people

English as the language of the boardroom

Writing English for global business may be something you are doing by choice. Sometimes, though, having to use English may be an unexpected development within a company. There was a movement in the late 1990s among various leading German companies, including Siemens and Hoechst, for executives to adopt English not only for external global communication but for internal business too. Indeed, the practice of designating English as the language of the boardroom is becoming increasingly widespread around the world.

Many cultures see that English is a language where it is relatively easy to pinpoint exactly the right word for any given situation. Its accessibility is a great advantage and as a result it predominates in the business world today.

Mergers and acquisitions and other developments

There are scenarios where businesses may expectedly, or unexpectedly, have to write in English. Mergers and acquisitions may take staff by surprise and require them to develop new skills. What if you are a non-NE writer who suddenly has to write in English but really do not want to? You are being asked to step completely out of your comfort zone.

So how do people react to this? Well, naturally enough, in different ways. Some people feel that if this is what it takes to get on, so be it. Some will be actively against it. And others will feel uncomfortable about being put in a position that they feel is by definition alien.

As a manager be aware of this. Lead by example – be seen to be writing effective English yourself. And offer support and training for your teams, so that they can write effective English too.

Helping you communicate across borders without building frontiers

As you will be using English in order to operate globally, your counterparts in other countries must understand you in the same way that you are understood at home. Search for ways to make the task easier for all.

How? Well, you have goals to achieve. So why create unnecessary problems by using over-complicated grammatical forms? Esperanto was specifically devised as an international language for common communication – and has a simplified grammatical base for that very reason. But Esperanto did not capture people's imaginations; instead, English has surged ahead in popular use. As English can also allow great simplicity, use it simply!

But this in no way equates to dumbing down or speaking down to people. It is more about realizing that, in business, time is money – for readers and writers alike.

How intercultural networking, socializing and training can help

Although this book is about writing, I do stress how important it can be for you to encourage intercultural networking. You will learn communication tips to help with your writing. So it is good to gain some awareness of how differing cultures intuitively choose English words.

Compare and contrast these two styles of written English. They are by two non-NE writers from different cultural backgrounds and refer to the same situation:

'We have a problem here and you need to fix it fast.'

'It seems there may be a systems failure. It would appear to be something that needs corrective action.'

How does it help to understand their backgrounds in order to deal with their writing? Well, the many multinational companies who have used my tips find that where readers are aware of writers' differing backgrounds when they write English, they are likely to be:

- less offended by extremely direct exchanges;

- less puzzled by deferential language where people do not appear willing to take the lead on decisions;

■ less frustrated by hierarchical language where a writer will only deal with a chief executive;

■ less bemused by overly polite language.

Checklist: practical solutions to help

Ask yourself:

Do I/we encourage cross-cultural socializing?

Do I/we encourage cross-cultural networking?

Do I/we offer internal or external company training in cross-cultural communication needs?

Is there anything else I/we could be doing in this connection in order to improve business writing in English?

Cultures that are accustomed to say yes

When writing English for global business, we need to be aware that in some cultures, writers will imply yes when they mean no. They may agree to things that are impossible. They may take on work that is impossible. All of this because their culture does not make them feel comfortable saying no – because:

■ they may feel they will appear unprofessional and lose face as a result;

■ they may feel they will be seen as uneducated and foolish if they do not understand;

- they may feel they will be judged to be lacking in resilience;
- they may prefer to avoid disagreement.

Case study

The problem

A major multinational company providing household products globally was experiencing what it perceived as problems with cross-cultural written exchanges. It was simply taking too long to get the results needed. What could be done? How could the company's written communications better draw out the information needed – and sooner rather than later?

The solution

We identified that it could be as simple as asking the right questions to elicit the relevant answers. Staff were shown how to avoid writing closed questions in e-mails (these are questions that typically lead to a yes/no or simple factual answer) and instead use open questions such as 'Why?' or 'How?'. The person being asked these would then have to reply in more than one word and would hopefully give a full and informative answer.

Examples to help you know what to write are:

Closed questions:

'Please can you complete this project by the 31st of this month?'

'Is the presentation ready?'

Open questions:

'What do you need to do to complete this?'

'What do you think?'

'How did this happen?'

'What further information would be useful to you?'

Summarizing questions:

These are also a useful tool to check that people from different cultures do understand one another. For example: 'Can we confirm: are we in agreement that this project will be brought forward one month?'

Cultures that are accustomed to say no

We have looked at closed questions such as 'Please can you let me have this information tomorrow?' Some cultures find saying no is easy, and they may see it as quite all right, and indeed efficient, simply to write 'No' in reply to the enquiry.

What they probably will not realize is that readers from 'yes' or 'maybe' cultures may be affronted by this. The response 'no' is not only inefficient in their opinion (because they need reasons why), it is also likely to have offended them, and totally unnecessarily.

Look at how easily the message can be adapted to suit both cultures:

'I'm afraid I cannot get the information to you tomorrow, as it is still being prepared. Will the day after tomorrow be all right?'

The person in the 'no' culture has not had to alter their stance in the sense that they are not sending the information tomorrow. But there is a shift in tone: they are giving reasons. In addition, they are making some effort to empathize: to check out the other person's feelings about this.

Help your staff

They may have general concerns

Many people dislike having to write in business, even in their own language. Even taking mergers and so on out of the equation, non-NE speakers may not actually want to write in English as a foreign language. If you manage multi-cultural teams, training may be key to success.

However, not everyone welcomes training. Some people do: they know there is power through knowledge. They see proficiency in business English as a powerful tool to speed their promotion prospects. Other staff will feel differently. English writing training is just another chore to add to their already demanding workload. Some will feel out-and-out antagonistic. Why should they have to write in English?

Understand that to succeed you must communicate the reason why English is essential in your business. You will help staff understand if you explain:

- It makes business communication quicker and cheaper to use English as a lingua franca.

- Knowing how to speak and write English is a key (and transferable) skill because most international written and online communication today is in English.

A tip: giving reasons why something should be done is key to success in all aspects of your business writing in English.

The skills crisis and business English writing

A skilled workforce is fundamentally important to any company's current and ongoing success. Managers often report that the most important attributes needed in new staff are:

- a willingness to learn;

- a good work ethic;

- the ability to work in teams.

As e-mail is by far the most prevalent form of business writing today (both internally and externally), the potential for mistakes or misunderstandings is arguably far greater than it used to be. It is hardly surprising that poor writing is part of the problem generically called 'the skills crisis'. It is a significant global problem.

How do we measure 'adequate business English writing?'

Simply acknowledging the problem is not the end of the story. Managers need to identify and nurture talent within their teams. One easy way of doing this is to unlock their employees' word power potential. But how?

One way would be to evaluate if everyone is performing adequately in their business writing. But what does 'adequately' mean? The box gives an example for you to think about.

Case study

A Dutch company once told me that everyone in the company had to undertake regular written business English assessments.

I asked what a good assessment mark would be and the managing director looked at me with surprise. Everyone naturally achieves 90 per cent and above, he said. It never occurred to him to set the bar higher. That is why my question puzzled him.

Now, if in your company you were giving say, marks out of 10 in written business English assessments, would it be acceptable if everyone had a pass mark of 5 or 6? Or should it be 7 or 8? Would 9 be unattainable, 10 unrealistic?

If English writing skills are important for taking your business forward, it is an interesting question for you to think about.

Why pay twice?

If your organization needs to write in English and your staff are highly skilled in doing so, you reduce the cost of managers constantly supervising their efforts. Why pay twice for one piece of work? Indeed, why pay the higher price for a manager's input when they could be freed up to do the work they are really paid to do?

And it certainly should not be you who has to oversee everyone's English writing on a daily basis!

Diversity in writing: key points to consider

Diversity in writing is something all managers need to address. I mention it here because it will make writing English for business even more of a challenge for some writers.

If you are in a larger company with a strong diversity agenda, you may be more aware of what follows. If not, you too need to know the facts.

Diversity in learning in the workplace involves challenges, of which dyslexia is one. Although certain writing mistakes result from some staff not applying themselves fully to the task in hand, other staff will work differently, through necessity. They will find writing intrinsically difficult and they will need to use different coping strategies – and have appropriate support – to deliver results. So in the interests of productivity, managers need to be aware how best to nurture all their employees' differing learning abilities and competencies.

Some indicators to look out for, where dyslexic staff may need your positive support and encouragement to write English (and the list is by no means exhaustive), are:

■ Poor handwriting, which dyslexic people sometimes use to hide their difficulties with spelling.

■ They may try to keep to the same formats, to keep to constants that they know.

■ They may have difficulty remembering language-based information such as instructions, or they may find it difficult to copy from a board or flipcharts.

■ They may be embarrassed when you correct them – so be sensitive to this and never allow yourself to be misinterpreted as picking on them because of their dyslexia (which in fact may not be diagnosed).

It is also good for you to be aware of other challenges, such as colour blindness or Irlen's syndrome, in which a person sees texts in swirls or in which words 'jump' and where closed letters seem to be infilled with black, and so on.

By the way, I do not agree with managers striking through their employees' writing with 'red pen corrections' or highlighting mistakes in any other heavy-handed manner. It often causes resentment. Managers should be offering support. It is true to say that yes, sometimes staff will make mistakes – there can be no other word for it. A lot of readers will react badly to these mistakes. Managers do need to intervene in these instances, but there are definitely right ways and wrong ways of doing this. But other than in matters of punctuation and grammar, managers can oversimplify when they say that one way is right and another wrong.

Your checklist for action

- Understand the importance of business English writing in terms of business performance, and assess the standards you need to set.

- Nurture your employees' communication skills generally.

- Gauge the impression your company needs to make to foster positive outcomes.

- Be aware that belonging to different cultures can have an impact on writers' communication styles when writing English.

- Be aware of other factors that can impact on a person's business English writing and which may require further support.

3

Why we communicate commercially

Businesses often underestimate the importance of written communication skills as an integral part of their total communication package. For some reason, writing can be viewed as too much of a 'soft skill' to justify on-the-job training. This book demonstrates how short-sighted this view can be. Using the power of this essential (and basically free) resource can dramatically take companies forward, helping them achieve many objectives faster.

Why we write in business

There are many reasons why we write in business, so it makes sense to identify and prioritize these. That's why at the outset of my training workshops I always ask people, 'Why do you need to write in your business?' And I mean this in both an individual and team sense.

My clients cover a whole host of companies from diverse cultural backgrounds, and naturally with differing objectives. I ask them to record on a flipchart why they need to write. Interestingly, they almost always begin the list with 'To give information and to record facts'. Even though there may be chief executives and sales managers among them, many end the list there. Only when I say that there must be other reasons as well do they rack their brains and then add other writing objectives, such as 'To engage interest, to involve readers, to persuade and to sell'.

Only one person has ever spontaneously written 'To eat, breathe and live our vision' and that was a relatively junior employee of a national charity. She had not been brainwashed: she believed in the vision. I really feel that this is something we can all learn from.

The preoccupation with writing as a tool simply to record information tells us a lot about the lack of awareness of how powerful writing English for business can be.

Why are we in business? Surely it is to make a livelihood by providing information or products or services to people who want or need them.

The written word is uncompromising: we have to get it right. Without the clues that body language give, without the give and take we allow the spoken word (we can question if we are not sure – and the spoken word does not have to be grammatically perfect), we judge written words for what they are. Whatever you write in your business English is frozen in time, so to speak. It represents you and your company for what it is.

Effect on performance

This book is about helping you focus on getting your writing in English right, as a high commercial priority. As a manager you may be investing heavily in people, projects and infrastructure, yet still fail to make the connection that your written words can be both the inspiration and the driving force that gets things done.

I remember my school motto well: 'Not words but deeds'. It was inspirational but does not sit so well in a business context. Deeds are not the whole story; in today's global marketplace we absolutely need spoken and written words as well. Indeed, even early caveman and cavewoman relatively soon figured out that words helped develop the deeds they were first primed to carry out. Actions could be described to structure a whole programme of events and also to involve others outside the direct group.

It does not take a giant leap to make relevant connections with the business world today. Of course we need to get our actions and our spoken words right. Yet to a large degree it is our written English words that help us:

- organize and record;

- cascade information;

- refine and update on an ongoing basis;

- team-build;

- inspire these actions.

This book may bring you an unexpected bonus. If you are not a native English writer, you may want to evaluate how effectively you write in your own language too – ironically, through the medium of this book about writing English for business!

Ideal communication

It will never be possible to write a recipe for ideal communication, but we can work towards a notion of optimal communication by ensuring that:

> The correct, concise, current message is sent out to a primary receiver, then onwards without distortion to further receivers to generate the required response.

When we write something to a primary receiver that is purely for information, all we need is that this receiver notes the correct message and our correct tone. If, however, we write to sell or persuade, then we are looking for the receiver(s) to respond not just favourably to our style but to act in response in the way and at the time we desire.

Our writing should actively enable this through the formula we design. So it is crucial that it can be understood by all who read it. It is essential that it cannot be misinterpreted or distorted by receivers who may send this message on to others (possibly without our knowledge). I also include 'current' in the formula because writers often forget to update messages when events, dates or other considerations may have changed. Companies lose efficiency this way.

The Word Power Skills system: four easy steps to success

The experience I have gained over the years in helping companies of all types and sizes communicate effectively shows that a systematic approach is always going to yield the best results. The more I help companies gain improved results in all their writing, the more I realize that rigour and consistency in approach really yield dividends.

Let me now introduce the system that you will find used throughout this series of books to encapsulate the key messages. It goes like this:

Step 1

Be correct:

- Know what your writing needs to achieve, alongside what your company needs to achieve.

- Match reader and customer expectations.

- Ensure that your writing is free of mistakes.

Your business communication will fail if you get your basics wrong.

Step 2

Be clear:

- Use plain English and express facts as simply as possible.

- Edit so that your main points are easily understood.

Confused messages undermine your objectives. They can lose you custom too.

Step 3

Make the right impact:

- Use the right words and layout to get noticed for the right reasons.

- Use the right style to present yourself and your company well.

- Create opportunities.

The right impact differentiates you from competitors and helps bring about the replies you need.

Step 4

Focus on your customers:

- Use words that focus on your readers and customers, and empathize with them.

- Use positive, proactive words where possible.

- Avoid words that put up barriers, and try to avoid jargon.

Use these words to satisfy and, if possible, delight your customers.

Correct for purpose: your mission, vision and values

It is not just your sales literature that should include positive messages about what you sell. So too should your company mission, vision, values or equivalent. Let's focus first on Step

1 in the system: checking that your writing is correct on all levels. This means correct in the sense that readers should not be able to find any mistakes, but correct also in being fit for purpose and meaningful. Finally, and at the very least, it means that it meets readers' expectations.

A number of companies I have helped now realize that:

- Their original mission, vision, values or equivalent have not made complete sense, not only in English but even in their original language (if different).

- These were never updated as circumstances changed.

- Staff were not aware of them.

- Staff did not understand their relevance to daily performance.

These companies can now see that if the starting point from which all corporate communication leads is wrong, then this adversely affects all subsequent communication.

At Step 1, you need to express actively and accurately what your organization does, how it does it better than the rest, at the right price, and in the right way for your customers' needs.

So do reflect before you choose the words in English that highlight all these aspects to optimum effect. Develop pride and then express pride. For example, you could swap this flat, lacklustre sentence ...

'Founded in 2001, we are looking to consolidate in the next five years.'

... with this:

'Building on our success since 2001, we are going for significant growth in the next five years.'

Yes, there are a few more words in the second version, but notice how the extra words add value.

This leads me to some key messages:

- In business every word we write should add value.

- If a word does not add value, consider cutting it out.

- If the words we write do not add value, then add ones that will.

Quality in business English

Let's address another aspect of Step 1, mistake-free writing, and let's look at your position regarding this, which the following scenarios will help you identify.

Mistakes in general

'Whats wrong with errers, if I do my job well?' someone might ask. And that really is the crux of the matter: will readers actually think you do your job well if they see mistakes? It is an unfortunate fact that if you make written mistakes, some readers will focus on these.

You may have seen the two deliberate mistakes: 'Whats' for 'What's' and 'errers' for 'errors'. Did you? If so, did you focus on them? Readers do – and, whether we like it or not, they can make value judgements such as 'This writer is not professional.' Whether it is fair or not, customers and bosses tend to view mistakes in English as direct evidence of sloppy business performance. External customers in particular can point the finger of blame at a company as a whole, and not just at the individual writer who may be responsible.

What is more, mistakes in your English writing are not just about poor spelling, grammar and punctuation. Mistakes can be a direct result of staff not thinking logically or anticipating likely outcomes each time they send out a written message.

Getting your English right can also be about understanding how to write positive messages that cut out jargon, ambiguity and rudeness. Even when you have to communicate negative messages, there are better ways and there are worse ways of doing this, as you will be seeing by now.

Your English writing can determine whether you make a great impact or a damaging impact, whether you win or lose custom, whether you foster goodwill or alienate those you should be supporting.

The good news? If poor writing is endemic in the workplace and causes confusion, misunderstandings or missed opportunities, then it is easy to see how great writing will set you and your company apart.

Mistakes by others that impact on us

Here are two real-life examples of problems companies have experienced as a result of the writing mistakes of others.

1. I once took up a company's offer to have a database entry on my company's services included in a Europe-wide guide. It was run by a reputable international trade organization and I sent my fully correct advertisement for inclusion. Unfortunately, the organization retyped my copy incorrectly and, without offering me a proof to check, published a mistakes-riddled version. Unknown to me, this had been listed publicly for one month before I received the invoice for payment.

Can you imagine my reaction when I found out? Displeased, to say the least. And do you think I paid the company's invoice? No, I did not. The company concerned had to make the invoice void (so losing income), had to retype a correct version of the database entry, then publicize this and bear an additional cost in so doing.

Although I had no account to pay, I still paid a high price in terms of loss of professional credibility, on an international scale. This was particularly disastrous in view of the nature of my business. Their mistake ultimately reflected on me, rather than on them.

What did I learn from this? It taught me never to make assumptions that my correct writing will be copied correctly by others. It also taught me to expressly state to any advertiser that no copy of mine may be published before I see a proof for my personal vetting.

2. The authorities at a major airport decided to run a customer feedback survey to see how they could improve their services to customers. They outsourced the survey to an agency and were greatly disappointed at some of the responses they received. Why? Because there were many negative reactions that were nothing directly to do with the airport authorities: they were in response to typographical errors made by the printer of the survey forms. Many customers were sufficiently irritated by what they perceived as unprofessionalism to respond critically – and not necessarily mention other aspects about the airport's operation that the survey had hoped to address.

Yet a lesson was learnt by the authorities: although the mistakes were not theirs, they still reflected on them rather than on the agency. In future, they knew that their communications could never be fully outsourced: they, as the clients, would have to retain the ultimate responsibility.

They also realized that readers often react negatively to written mistakes. They acknowledged readers' frequent perception that writers who make mistakes do not care about quality or professionalism – or even about customers in general.

Quality: the debate is on

A newly appointed non-English plant manager in a major oil company had a team of Asian and European staff, none of whom was a native English speaker. His own spoken English was not fluent, but he felt that he was more fluent than the rest. When it came to writing, once again he felt that, although far from perfect, he was still better than most. So in his view he was succeeding in his use of English.

Interestingly, I have come across a similar view in a UK company, whose managing director compared his company's business writing performance alongside that of its direct UK competitors. So here we are talking about one company, comprising only native English speakers, comparing its performance with others, also comprising only native English speakers.

The managing director confirmed that his company did occasionally make mistakes in their business writing. After all, he explained, 'To err is human.' This is an English expression that means 'People will always make mistakes.' He went on to add that, as his company's direct competitors made more errors, he was satisfied that his company was 'better than the rest'.

As a manager, would you agree with this viewpoint? Should quality in English writing be relative or absolute in value? It is for you and your customers to decide.

Accountability

Many companies have renamed an attribute they may previously have called 'responsibility' to 'accountability'. It is an interesting change of word, not least because of nuances in meaning in English. You see, accountability is both the requirement to justify actions or decisions (responsibility) but can also denote culpability or liability. In this respect, the word can appear to have rather more negative connotations than 'responsibility'. So whereas companies may write, 'Our staff take pride in their accountability', it is very noticeable that sometimes staff feel rather apprehensive about that claim.

Define your English meanings regularly

If this strikes a chord, define what your organization means by accountability. Understand how you need to explain the use of the word to staff and get them on board. Make sure that this word (as with every word you use in English) is not just an 'empty' word – used without the correct meaning. Simply by taking time to define your meaning each time you choose a new word to describe your values and vision, you enhance the likelihood of the outcomes you need.

Your checklist for action

■ You need to customize your writing in English for your business vision and values, and for your daily business goals.

■ Understand that the right message + business focus = personal + team success + corporate gains.

■ Define your English meanings regularly, particularly when company vision is involved.

■ Each time you start a new piece of writing, focus on getting it right and understand what quality means in terms of business English writing (free of mistakes on all levels).

■ Use the four-step guide to premier business writing as a tool for every aspect of your English writing performance.

4

Word Power Skills 2.0: interacting with readers as customers

The importance of Word Power Skills 2.0

Have you heard of Web 2.0? In essence, this is about creating interactive, interrelating content for the web, so that the content does not lead to a dead end but leads from one thing to another in as unified a way as possible. In a business context, it is one further manifestation of the notion of the cycle of business that I introduced in the Preface to this book.

Now I want to introduce you to using Word Power Skills 2.0 in everything you write in English for business. Word Power Skills 2.0 means using the same principles of interactivity to create writing that speaks directly to customers. Why should this interactivity stop at writing for the web?

Be one step ahead. Make sure that:

- you apply the same principles to all your English business writing;

- your letters, e-mails, progress reports and so on follow this essential route of enabling interaction with readers;

- once you have made contact in any way with readers as customers, you use your English to keep them informed and involved – in short, keep them in the loop.

That is why this chapter focuses on empathy: putting yourself in your customers' position when you write.

How you view readers

Ask yourself these questions:

- Who are your internal and external readers?

- Do you view both groups as customers, as many companies do?

- Is your goal to satisfy customers? Or to delight them? (I will be elaborating on this shortly.)

- When you write, do you tend to write the minimum or the maximum?

- Do you write to protect yourself against future repercussions?

- Do you write to answer questions as well as anticipate possible questions?

- Do you write to keep readers away or to get them on board?

- Are you reluctant to write or do you even dread writing in English?

- Do line managers expect to help?

Could you help improve the way your company writes? Could you do this as an individual or could you work with others to make a difference in this area?

Constructions that may confuse your readers and customers

A very effective way of helping both NE and non-NE readers understand your messages is simply to avoid wherever possible the following two writing forms.

Double negatives; negatives versus positives

If two negative words written in the same sentence relate to the same thing, then the meaning becomes positive. For example:

'It is impossible not to like her' = 'It is not possible to find a person who does not like her.'

The two negatives cancel each other out so that the meaning becomes positive; in effect: 'Everybody likes her.'

'It is unlikely that the situation will not improve' = 'It is likely that the situation will improve.'

You can see how much better it is to use the positive version at the outset. It is far better psychologically and it is far better than making your readers try to work out the meaning – and maybe fail.

But if you use only one negative, the meaning remains negative: 'This does not preclude the installation of such appliances elsewhere.'

The use of the negative here does make the sentence quite cumbersome, even for a native English reader. It becomes much easier to read when rewritten positively: 'Such appliances can be installed elsewhere.'

Another example is: 'The project was unsuccessful.' Even though this is perfectly acceptable, you may still find that non-NE readers find 'The project failed' easier to understand.

Similarly, they are likely to find it easier to understand 'He had some anxious moments waiting for the results' rather than 'It was not without some anxious moments that he waited for the results.'

Active and passive

There is a difference between active and passive voice in English writing that you need to understand. The passive voice is more likely to confuse readers, so business writers today tend to avoid it where possible. Let me outline the difference.

The active voice is where the subject does the action; for example: 'The management team held a special meeting to discuss the crisis.'

The passive voice is where the subject of the active clause becomes secondary, where it is acted upon or receives the action. Often the word 'by' is added, as we can see in the following sentence: 'A special meeting was held by the management team to discuss the crisis.' It has taken two more words to write the passive and, in a sense, the people (the management team) seem secondary to the meeting. The meaning is still clear enough, though. But what often happens in writing the passive voice is that the subject tends to be left out altogether: 'A special meeting was held to discuss the crisis.'

This leaves readers wondering who actually held the meeting. Even if it was obvious at the time to that target audience, some months later will it still be obvious?

Another very common example of the passive voice is: 'A safety helmet should be worn at all times when any work is undertaken on this site.' People tend to use this style on autopilot, so to speak. It is actually far clearer to convert it to the active voice: 'You must wear a safety helmet at all times when you work on this site.'

To be fair, there are occasions when use of the passive serves a good business purpose, as the next two sentences show:

'The director made a mistake in this calculation.'
'A mistake has been made in this calculation.'

In the first sentence the finger of blame is pointed at the director, who clearly made a mistake. In the second sentence the passive means that the reader does not know who made the mistake. This can be a useful writing mode for organizations that do not believe in a blame culture. But it will not work where the reader needs to know who is accountable. So, overly passive writing can present problems. Readers can falsely assume that, because the subject (the doer) is hidden, nobody needs to do anything as a result.

Simplicity can impress

People often react negatively to what they see as pomposity in others. Pomposity often manifests itself in verbose, over-complicated sentences. In fact, if we look at just one sector in the UK, we will find that one quarter of all complaints received by the Law Society in recent years relate to solicitors' poor communication skills.

Their customers have reacted with irritation, even downright annoyance, to letters that they find hard to understand, patronizing and unhelpful. The legal profession realizes that it has to make a choice. Although it may not be the stark choice that some professions have to make, of 'adapt or perish', many members have decided to change. Out has gone archaic Latin terminology and in comes writing plain English, as clients increasingly demand.

However complicated the subject matter, business clients pay for experts:

- to shoulder the burden of writing and know what to do;

- to keep them informed (in writing) about the essential points, in simply expressed facts.

Writing customer service

When you shop, how often have you been treated badly by shop assistants? The chances are that your statistics for this will be high. Why should this be? After all, retailers, in common with many other businesses, risk losing significant custom as a result of poor customer care. Many are prepared to focus on product and price – but not on customers as people rather than inanimate 'footfall', a term that reduces people to the numbers entering a shopping area within a specific timescale.

Today's customers are increasingly assertive. They expect extra benefits, in the form of better service: an intangible that can differentiate between providers. So if you can commit to and deliver premier customer care, it can put you in a strong position to get ahead.

Providing everything else is right, one way you can do this is by expressing customer care in the virtually free, highly visible medium that is your English business writing.

Case study

The customer care ladder: a writing strategy to help

I originally devised the three-step strategy that follows to help an American company that was going global. Their company ethos was very strong but they faced a new challenge: how could they explain it in accessible English to the multi-cultural teams they would be inducting into the company?

The system worked successfully and easily for them and I am delighted to say it has been adopted by a great many multinational companies since.

The customer care ladder

Climbing the first rung on the ladder

- You will never ascend the first rung on the ladder if you do not mean customer care and do not express it.

- You can take your first step up the ladder if you express the language of customer care, but you will get stuck if you do not mean it.

- You can take your first step up if you mean customer care but do not express it.

Climbing the second rung on the ladder

- You can climb the second rung on the ladder when you express and mean the words of customer care.

■ At this point you get the words and sentiments exactly right for the customer(s) in question.

Climbing the third and subsequent rungs

■ You can now continue ascending until you reach the top of the ladder, the point at which you exceed customers' expectations.

■ You do this when you anticipate your customers' needs and you meet those needs.

■ You also go the extra step and delight your customers when you meet needs maybe before your customers have even thought of them.

You see, the higher you go, the more competitors you will leave behind. Their complacency holds them back. You reach the top when you enable your customers to feel the wow factor; it is this that will set you ahead of the rest. Surely that is where you want to be?

Unclear English can distract you from your goal

Here is a very common problem you are almost sure to encounter. It happens when various people of different proficiency levels in writing English get involved in stages of a specific task. It can often mean writers focus on meaning – to the point of forgetting their ultimate business goal. The goal, that is, of developing great and sustainable relationships with customers by communicating and delivering customer delight.

The scenario described in the following case study demonstrates what I mean. The company names are fictitious but the circumstances occur time after time. Read the e-mail strand and evaluate how effective the writing is.

Case study

A native English-speaking global retailer from ABC Inc urgently needed a consignment of shoes to be shipped from China by China Xpress Shipping. He had placed a time-specific order with his regular supplier, Speedi Freight Solutions, a European shipping company.

The two companies corresponded by e-mail in English, as is customary in the world of transportation. As the deadline for delivery of the shoes was approaching, the retailer e-mailed the shipping company to check that all was in order. The following e-mails ensued, in date order:

Date: 12 January
From: ABC Inc
To: Speedi Freight Solutions
Subject: our express order 123

Juan
We would like your assurance that this shipment will be with us by the close of business Monday, 23 February, as agreed.
Regards
Peter

Date: 12 January
From: Speedi Freight Solutions
To: ABC Inc
Subject: your express order 123

Peter
I am checking current progress and will get back to you with this confirmation.
Kind regards
Juan

Date: 12 January
From: Speedi Freight Solutions
To: China Xpress Shipping
Subject: goods consignment CX102

Li
Our clients need this order fast. Is it on its way?
Thks
Juan

Date: 13 January
From: China Xpress Shipping
To: Speedi Freight Solutions
Subject: Re: goods consignment CX102

Juan
Long waits experienced at port due public holiday. Consignment got
priority in line, despatch arrive as soon as possible.
Li

Date: 14 January
From: Speedi Freight Solutions
To: China Xpress Shipping
Subject: goods consignment CX102

Li
I do not quite understand what you mean. Do you mean the consignment
is still held up at the port? Or has it been held up at the port – and is now
on its way? If so, when did it leave and when will it arrive?
Thks
Juan

Date: 18 January
From: China Xpress Shipping
To: Speedi Freight Solutions
Subject: Re: goods consignment CX102

Juan
Sorry for delay in replying – back from public holiday today. Consignment
delayed but port authorities doing all possible to help ... delivery
deadline should be ok. I confirm in a couple of days.
Li

Date: 20 January
From: China Xpress Shipping
To: Speedi Freight Solutions
Subject: Re: goods consignment CX102

Juan
Yes, order on track. Delivery date 23 February ok.
Li

Date: 20 January
From: Speedi Freight Solutions
To: ABC Inc
Subject: your express order 123

Peter
Further to your e-mail enquiry of 12 January, I can confirm that this
order will be with you by the close of business Monday, 23 February,
as agreed.
Kind regards
Juan

What are your thoughts on the e-mail communications in the
box? Think about what ABC Inc were looking for in their
original e-mail. Did Speedi Freight Solutions deal with this in
the best way? Or did they get distracted along the way? If so,
why?

These e-mails show a pattern I see all too often when English
is used in global business writing:

When the English is unclear, it can mean that the reader takes
longer to deal with issues – because they may have to dig deep
to discover what the writer means. In this particular example,
Speedi Freight Solutions had to exchange a further e-mail
with China Xpress Shipping just to find out what they were
actually saying. Because there was a public holiday in China,
this delayed the outcome further.

When e-mail is used routinely because NE speakers and writers feel more comfortable in this medium, this can also take longer than picking up the telephone (although there can also be problems with time zones in this respect).

It actually took Juan – and by implication Speedi Freight Solutions as a whole – eight days to get an informed reply back to their client in view of these factors.

In this instance, the communication glitch was relatively acceptable – in the sense that the client's consignment was likely to arrive on time. But what if the order had been delayed past the due date? How would Speedi Freight Solutions have had time to make alternative arrangements?

Do you think ABC Inc were impressed by Speedi Freight Solutions' speed of response to their enquiry?

Would you agree that the language glitch meant that Speedi Freight Solutions was distracted from one of the essential goals in business: keeping one's focus on the customer?

Truly customer-centred writing means that Juan should have kept Peter informed sooner rather than later. I think he should have sent an interim reply. He then should have explained why there was a delay in getting the answer. (Even better, he should have had the answers himself!)

Cultural differences in the choice of English for customer service

It comes more easily to some cultures to serve than to others. And it can be more difficult for some to express customer service in words. How do you feel, for example, about the expression 'Have a nice day'?

If you think customer care is good for business, then why not identify ways to express this in your business English writing? Avoid the 'language of disservice' at all costs. What is this? Well, here is a starter list:

- Letting readers see spelling and grammatical errors in your business English.

- Writing the wrong English words (maybe also in the wrong place and at the wrong time).

- Conveying the wrong sentiments by choosing overly direct English expressions such as 'don't', 'can't' or 'won't' where these are inappropriate.

These English expressions can all contribute to a 'do not care' scenario. Readers generally do not like to see them, although, as you saw earlier, some cultures will find these words quite acceptable – and may need to understand that for other cultures they are not.

As another example, expressions such as 'We note your complaint' may be acceptable to some; others will be incensed that the writer has not expressed greater empathy, such as 'We are so sorry to hear about the problems you have encountered.'

You may want to ask around your organization and identify what English words will express the right attitude towards your customers – by culture and by sector, if need be. You could make a note of them in the following box so that you build them into your writing.

Tone

Chapter 9 deals with the crucial aspect of tone in English in e-mails but it is true to say that poor tone undermines all aspects of business writing, particularly customer service.

Express thanks in your business English writing

When you are in a shop and you decide to buy something, it is good news for that retailer. So as the consumer, what do you expect when you go to the cash desk to pay? That the cashier will be courteous? That they will say 'Thank you'? Most people expect this as a minimum expression of customer care. What if the cashier is 'busy' chatting to a colleague and apparently cannot be bothered to serve you; what does this express? Or if you pay and are not thanked?

Most people get irritated (even the mildest-mannered can be surprised at their annoyance) if they are unacknowledged.

Luckily the opposite is true: we are happy when retailers create positive customer experiences. So why, when it comes to business writing, do organizations not routinely express thanks for buyers' custom? I do. My invoices always end: 'With thanks for your custom'.

Do consider whether you could actively thank every customer in writing for their custom, if you do not already do so. You may be pleasantly surprised at the results.

Dealing with written complaints

Once you understand how to analyse what your own words are saying, you are in a better position to analyse writing around you. It is immensely helpful when you deal with written complaints. You can more easily understand how these do not necessarily mean lost custom. Rather, it can be useful feedback, to convert to a positive outcome.

It is certainly a better scenario than where a dissatisfied customer does not tell you about their dissatisfaction, but tells others instead. Bad news certainly spreads fast – and your competitors can win new business at your expense.

Understand what has caused the customer to write to complain

If you want to convert a customer's written complaint in English into a successful outcome, step one can be to understand that something has gone wrong. Maybe an order was incorrect. Maybe the customer has perceived poor service some other way. There can be problems even where the native language is used. So imagine how many more problems may arise when there are problems with writing English too.

Be aware that these problems can arise where writers take standard expressions from English textbooks and fail to customize their use appropriately.

Look at the example in the box.

Case study

Some time ago I bought a new washing machine made by a leading manufacturer. I soon noticed, to my horror, that my washing was getting torn by the machine. So what did I do? I highlighted the problem in writing to the manufacturers.

At the very least, this is what I expected from them:

- A prompt acknowledgement of receipt of my complaint, if not a full reply by return.

- Some expression of empathy: 'We are sorry to hear about the problems' (whether or not the manufacturer was accountable).

- That someone from the company would make an appointment with me as soon as possible, to investigate the situation (my washing was being ruined, after all) and to put things right.

This is an extract from the written reply I actually received:

I am sorry to hear about the damage caused to your clothes during washing, but your (named brand) washing machine model has complied with all our standard checks.
I trust you find this information helpful.

The Manager
Customer Care Department (company name)

Can you imagine how I felt? I was already aggrieved – and this reply made me angrier. I no longer felt that the manufacturer would solve the problem, so the situation escalated. I knew my legal rights and said I would take the matter further. At that stage the manufacturer sent an engineer round to my house. He examined the machine, discovered that the washing drum was faulty and undertook to replace the machine with a new one, at no extra cost.

In fact, many consumers had this problem with this machine model. A national television programme had heard about this, and was championing consumers' rights in this connection. As you know, negative publicity travels fast because we tend to talk about it when a company has treated us badly.

So what does this mean for that company's reputation – and its sales? I will not buy from them again.

How did writing come into the picture? In these ways:

- I did not like their attitude in the way they wrote to me.

- I did not like the fact that they used a standard English ending – 'I trust you find this information helpful' – when it clearly was not!

- I did not like the fact that it took a long time to resolve an acute problem.

- But it did not take that company long to lose my custom: just one badly written letter did that.

When you have to deal with a written complaint, try to understand why that person is complaining. Make the effort and take the time to empathize, because the person you may see as an awkward customer may in fact be:

■ A confused reader, maybe even confused by your writing – especially if you are a non-NE speaker (and you are lucky that they have come back to you).

■ An irritated reader, because you may have wasted their time in a different way: for example, by failing to respond to their precise needs or requests for information.

■ Someone who is asking for your help in solving a problem – and may be frustrated by your failure to grasp this.

■ A reader who is annoyed that you do not seem to be treating them as a valued customer.

■ Someone who, although displeased with something about your company, still wants to do business with you (otherwise they would have walked away).

So when you reply in writing, see if you can design your English so that:

■ You can suggest a positive solution in a friendly, positive manner.

■ You can at least show that you care about the complaint, give reasons as to why the problem happened and affirm that you will try to ensure that the customer never has cause to make that or any complaint again.

■ Where the complaint is misdirected, point that out in a helpful way and try to direct the person to an organization or person who can perhaps help.

Your checklist for action

- Apply the concepts of Web 2.0 to create interactive English writing that speaks directly to your readers, sees things from their perspective and keeps them in the loop. Apply these principles in everything you write – not just your writing for the web. This is Word Power Skills 2.0.

- Understand that great writing does not just happen: you design it, so that it works for you and for your readers.

- Writing English for business needs to be results-focused to succeed.

- Understand how simplicity can impress and how to achieve this.

- Focus on your customers' concerns; address these in your writing and try to prevent them.

- Understand how standard expressions and words taken straight from English textbooks can be disastrous.

5

Adapt: stay ahead or stay behind

Identify the right words for today

Dinosaurs failed to survive because they were unable to adapt to a changing environment. Some businesses share something in common with those dinosaurs. To sustain success, you need to know when to adapt and innovate your business writing. But set the right limits, as ill-conceived change can be a recipe for disaster.

So question how best to use your business writing to promote your messages, your products and your services. How can I help you do this? Well, keep a checklist. Identify the right words for today by eliminating words and expressions from the past that have outlived their relevance and thus their usefulness. Let me give you an idea of what these may be.

Yesterday's words

'Dear Sirs' used to be a valid opening in business English correspondence, when writers assumed that companies were run by men, but has long since fallen out of favour. In a world that is increasingly 'politically correct' it can be a gaffe to assume that a company is necessarily headed by male bosses. This opening is still valid if that is the case, but if you have to write to a company and do not know to whom to address your letter, do try to find out before you start writing. Look at the company website or make a telephone call to check, if this is feasible. Otherwise, you could begin your letter or e-mail: 'Dear Sir or Madam'.

Here is an example of yesterday's writing. It is not meant to be part of any contract; it is purely advice from a project manager to their team:

> However, all those engaged in the aforementioned project are hereby advised that no amendment to the project requirements which entails an alteration to the overall project budget can be regarded as duly authorized unless it is issued in accordance with the procedures specified by the acting project manager.

It takes time for even a native reader to understand what this means, so imagine what it could be like for a non-native English reader. In simple terms, the essence of the message is:

> Note to project team
>
> If any changes to the budget are needed you must let me know, as I am the only person authorized to amend the existing arrangements.
> Many thanks
> (Name)

This second version is concise and includes a heading to high-light what it is about. It is just as accurate, so what was the advantage in creating the first, long-winded, old-fashioned version?

Further examples

In the sentences below, the old-fashioned English sentence is followed by its modern equivalent:

'We gladly await your instructions at your earliest convenience.' = 'We look forward to hearing your requirements in the near future.'

'Please sign the form attached hereunder and return this to the aforesaid address, in any event no later than seven days from now.' = 'Please sign the attached form and return this to us within the next seven days.'

'Please retain proof of purchase in the event of any requirement to exchange the merchandise or effect a refund at some subsequent stage.' = 'Please keep your receipt in case you wish to exchange your purchase or get a refund in the future.'

'You are required to refrain from smoking at all times.' = 'No smoking.'

'Do not extinguish your car lights in the tunnel.' = 'Keep your lights on in the tunnel.'

Identifying today's and tomorrow's words

Even these examples may have to change in time. The English language is changing and other things move on too. Business goals change as do organizations' visions and values. It means you need to update relevant information and cascade this throughout your organization. As your business evolves, you will also need to adapt your communication outwards to your external customers and suppliers. All your English writing must consistently relate to readers' needs and expectations.

Exercise

Have you an idea now of English words you use that you may now want to avoid? And of words that may have a more modern feel that you think you should be using?

Write them down now and carry on adding to the list in the future. Share your findings with colleagues and swap ideas.

Words to discard

Words to favour

Who to tell – and when to review

Sometimes you need to 'unlearn' things

You need to have an open mind in business and sometimes you need to 'unlearn' things. Maybe the way you were originally taught needs adapting, as I suggest in previous chapters. Maybe you were taught the wrong things; it could be that you write over-academically for business today. Maybe your English teacher taught you correctly how to use the passive voice – unaware that business today largely rejects this in favour of plain English, actively expressed.

So do identify where you need to 'unlearn' things. Sometimes you do this simply by observing the writing of others, where you sense they are getting it right. Up to a point, you can mirror their best practice. It can be an effective way of learning.

The i-generation: the impact on writing

If you are a member of the i-generation (one of the terms used to describe the generation that has grown up with the internet) you will know how your life can be centred on the web. What you may not have realized is the extent to which internet use today has impacted on the way we write English, as the predominant business (and social) language of the worldwide web:

> We are influenced by the way we see English written for the web and expect businesses generally to be using it that way.

If you stop to analyse them, information fast-load and over-load can have some very obvious consequences that may affect business performance. Among these we find:

- Often we do not to take as much time as we might like to think about information.

- We do not concentrate for any length of time; after a few seconds we expect to move on, maybe at a click of the mouse.

- As a result we may not be taking the action that we should.

Aspects of writing e-mails in English will be covered in Chapter 9 but I would just like to stress one important point here. It is about the very real need to present written facts in an easily (if not instantly) accessible format in as much of our business English writing as possible.

Modern readers increasingly expect your business English writing to:

- Edit out waffle.

- Highlight key messages.

- Use descriptive headings and subheadings where possible.

- Cut out overload but include signposting that points readers in the right direction so that they can access more information as necessary (so that in effect it is just a click away).

Most importantly, wherever possible let your business writing point out to readers the people in your organization who can help them further.

Updating

It is essential that you update details as necessary, although managing content can be an aspect of business English writing that managers frequently overlook. Yet feedback consistently shows that:

- Readers get annoyed if they inform companies of changes to their personal details but find that writers have not updated their records.

- Companies waste time and money sending messages to the wrong receivers.

- Companies waste time and money sending messages to the right receivers but at the wrong time.

- Failure to update (for example, website information with wrong details) may actually be viewed as misinformation, which can have far-reaching consequences.

Correct timing

I would like to pick up on one of the points just referred to. I recently received a mailing about an interesting event and was going to attend – until I discovered the event had already taken place. On another occasion, a major retailer advertised their one-off sale event in the national press on the day of the sale only. They made the assumption that if you buy a daily paper or pick up a free paper, you will read it early enough on the day to persuade you to visit the store.

But assumptions are bad news in every aspect of business writing: commuters may read newspapers first thing in the morning; other people may read newspapers only in the evening. Who is to say that evening readers are not also consumers? Yet this target audience has been lost: they cannot get to an event they do not know about. And not only has their spending potential been lost; their goodwill may be lost too if they feel they have missed any wonderful bargains on offer.

All any company has to do is place the advertisement at a realistic time before the event. This would not only better facilitate customer footfall and therefore sales, it would also promote better customer relations.

Indeed if the timing is wrong and it is the advertiser's lack of foresight that makes it so, you could call this an 'own goal'. Imagine how much more complicated timing can be when differing international time zones are involved. Know your target audience's profile before you write your English, because:

■ Writing well is not just about focusing on your English.

■ It is also about focusing on every aspect that will make your message succeed.

■ Businesses that make assumptions in their writing and assumptions about their readers are likely to get the wrong outcomes time after time.

Your checklist for action

■ Use the English language and style that are right for your business and your readers today – and understand the need to review this continuously.

■ 'Unlearn' outdated approaches to using English and discard them.

■ Recognize that the internet has fundamentally altered how we communicate and how we expect business English to be written.

■ Ensure that your communication in English is timely for your target audience (who may be in different time zones), and keep it current.

6

Time is money

What does this mean?

Case study

In one meeting attended by 10 delegates from five different countries, one of the delegates referred in his report to 'a lake of resources'. The remaining nine delegates (of whom two were English) did not question the reference. The native English speakers did not quite understand but they did not want to embarrass the writer by asking what he meant. Instead they discussed among themselves that it must mean 'an abundance of resources'.

But soon they became puzzled. Certain things people said made it seem that the 'lake of resources' was not very abundant after all. In fact, the meeting itself was not making much sense at all.

Eventually one delegate took the lead and asked the writer to explain what the 'lake' meant. Precious time had been wasted by the group trying to understand instead of asking right at the outset of the meeting: 'what does this mean?'

The answer the writer gave makes for a salutary lesson: he had intended to write 'lack of resources'. He had quite simply made a mistake in his written English.

Just imagine what the commercial consequences could be in certain situations, where your writing expresses almost the exact opposite of what you intended.

Complex writing isn't always apt – or clever

Sometimes, the more senior people become in an organization, the more complicated they make their writing. They can mistakenly think that this highlights their intelligence and sets them apart as cleverer than the rest.

But written English for global business today is unlikely to achieve our goals if it does not build bridges across cultures and develop sustainable working relationships with customers. To truly succeed, our writing needs to express that it is they who are valued.

Let the unicorns flourish

When I run workshops for my clients, I always ask them to look at external business writing that has grabbed their attention. In subsequent sessions we then discuss which aspects have impressed and why.

Case study

In one such session, a finance director from China brought in a financial article entitled 'Let the unicorns flourish', which he had particularly enjoyed reading, not least because of the 'poetic' language. It showed a mastery of English that impressed him greatly and that he considered entirely right for purpose.

It was an interesting point – and I was certainly intrigued by the title, as a unicorn is a mythical creature, usually represented as a horse with a single horn at the front of its head. So I could imagine that the article would be about something other than unit trusts and the like, which, as it turned out, was exactly what it was about.

I wondered how other target financial professionals I knew might react. Would it grab their attention and make them likely to read? I asked 10 of them what they thought. Their reactions were, broadly, 'This meant nothing to us; we didn't read on.' Interestingly though, where they saw more prosaic headlines such as 'Hedge funds crisis' or 'Managers to forego bonuses', they did read the articles that followed.

So one size is unlikely to fit all when it comes to writing English for business, though some approaches, such as prosaic and factual ones, are likely to have more common currency than others. The director from China and the unicorns feature writer were clearly both on the same wavelength, but the others I questioned were not. Much as some readers (including myself) will love classical, literary writing, it is best to use it sparingly in business and only where you absolutely know it will work.

If you need a dictionary to decipher almost every word, it is not the sort of language that will work for business. Why? Because:

- Firstly, time is money for all of us as readers, as well as writers.

- Secondly, if I am a manager who sees writing that I do not understand, I might pretend I do (especially when it has been written by another senior executive). I might falsely assume that everybody else understands, and that I would appear stupid if I did not. (Though what if the target audience do not understand it either?)

Let's consider an expression I have seen: 'heralding a new era'. Do you understand this? It sounds poetic and it sounds nice. However, if people do not understand what it signifies, then it simply is not worth using in a business context. Perhaps 'introducing a new age', though more prosaic, would be understood by more readers. This is a balancing act that you have to consider each time you write for a global audience.

Sense or nonsense

It is naturally essential to get your advertising campaigns in English right. Let's look at an example that springs to mind here. It concerns a glossy magazine advertisement for men's swimwear. A picture of swim shorts had a caption that made a memorable claim:

'Our swimwear plays harder, dries faster, in or out of water.'

Now what exactly does this mean? The swimwear 'plays'? So is it alive? And how does it play harder? It may dry fast out of water – but it dries fast in water? That is impossible. Yet that is the nonsense that the caption claims.

You could argue that it does not matter. It is only swimwear after all, so there is no big deal. But I think that there is an important issue here: I don't think that the copywriter necessarily realized that the claims were nonsense. In that case, it is a case of flawed logic, as opposed to simply writing zany English copy to grab readers' attention.

If our logic is seen to be flawed in our English, we undermine our own message. We can actually lose professional credibility. Our readers may ask themselves why they should ever believe anything this company says. Or they may wonder if the company thinks they are idiots.

Good transitions improve fluidity

When you incorporate fluidity in your writing by creating logical connections, you help readers move seamlessly from one paragraph to the next. Structured, coherent writing can actually give readers confidence in you.

Transitional words and phrases are an easy tool to help you achieve a technique that enables your executive writing to shine. To summarize, transitions help us show the relationships between one statement and subsequent ones. They can link paragraphs, point towards a bigger picture and can help lead readers to a logical conclusion. You will recognize many of them in this list of examples:

firstly;

secondly;

similarly;

what's more;

but;

although;

however;

whereas;

finally.

The additional point I would like to make is this. You can enhance your executive writing simply by knowing whether it could be better to discard certain 'academic' English transitional words such as:

notwithstanding;

henceforth;

furthermore;

nevertheless.

And instead use more modern English, such as:

despite;

as well;

yet.

The precise choice depends, as always, on your target readers.

English dictionary syndrome

There are two important messages here, for NE and non-NE writers alike.

When you seek vocabulary help from a dictionary or thesaurus, do not feel that you must choose the longest words and construct the most complicated sentences. This flies in the face of all the advice given in this book so far. Why prefer unnatural, oblique 'un-English' sentences that readers are unlikely to understand, and that sound unconvincing?

Examples are:

'It necessitates us acquiring a dozen people in addition in order to facilitate a positive functioning of this assignation.' (In plain English: 'We need 12 more people to make this project work.')

'It will ameliorate an already existent predicament.' (In plain English = 'The current situation will improve.')

Do not run before you can walk. Choose words you understand (and can pronounce!), because you will be noticed one hundred times more – and for the wrong reasons – if you use English words you do not understand or cannot pronounce if questioned.

Write a brief before you commit to action

People generally understand the importance of formal meeting notes (which are covered in Chapter 7) but can fail to see that some written record can be essential in informal meetings too. It can be inefficient in the extreme if you don't get people to agree to a written brief before you and they commit to action.

This is even more likely to happen in an informal meeting with non-NE speakers with differing levels of proficiency, and probably no designated chairperson (as would be the case in a formal meeting). There is a far greater chance that there may be some misunderstandings as to the action agreed, as well as to who will take which action, what is involved, the cost, the timescale, who will report on ongoing status and who will sign off.

The real-life example in the box illustrates this.

Case study

At one informal project managers meeting, nobody quite knew what action was needed between departments, and indeed between countries. One manager spontaneously offered to help a colleague sort this out after the meeting; something she subsequently regretted. She thought it had been agreed that the project needed an external assessment – and fast, so that the delivery would be on time.

She arranged the assessment and e-mailed everyone to keep them informed. The colleague she thought she was helping then e-mailed her tersely by return (copying in all the other managers), stating that she had no authority to do this. The assessment would incur an extra cost, not yet factored into the project – and only he could authorize this.

How do you think the two managers in this case study felt about each other as a result of what had happened?

Badly, is the answer. How do you think the remaining managers felt? Embarrassed.

Confirming the brief for an agreed course of action would have prevented these subsequent problems – and ill-feeling – from happening. The project manager in question could have e-mailed everyone straight after the meeting:

- capturing what she had felt had been agreed;

- setting out what she proposed to do next, the timing and the costs involved;

- getting the colleague she was directly helping to ask if he could cover these additional costs in the budget.

The burden of responsibility would have been on the others to agree or disagree with each action outlined, before she proceeded further. In instances such as this, written confirmation can be immensely valuable.

Before I leave this subject, it is helpful to keep the following in mind:

- Some cultures will sometimes switch from an ordinary (therefore official) conversation to an unofficial conversation, especially within informal meetings. The switch is sometimes obvious, sometimes not. In some cases you may discover that a conversation was, unknown to you at the time, unofficial.

▪ Some cultures may say 'yes' when they mean 'no'. They will agree to things that are impossible. They will take on work that is impossible. All because they can be afraid to say no.

When acronyms can become the problem

Acronyms were only ever intended to save time and make life easier. The original intention was that an acronym made an abbreviated word (formed by the initial letters of other words or sometimes of a compound noun) to make those words or nouns easier both to refer to and remember. That is why writers refer to the United Nations as the UN, the Organization of Petroleum Exporting Countries as OPEC, and the British Broadcasting Corporation as the BBC.

At the first use of an acronym in your writing, you do need to explain it. The convention is that you use the full name or words, then put the acronym in brackets after it; for example: World Health Organization (WHO). Then you can just use the acronym, as your readers can understand your meaning. In practice, however, writers very often offer no such explanation – and write in abundance on subjects that you simply cannot understand. It does not mean that you are not proficient in English. It means that they are being thoughtless.

Indeed, writers' thoughtless use (and overuse) of English acronyms can be where the business world goes crazy. The moment we have to ask 'What does this mean?' (if we are confident enough to admit we do not know) or 'Is this overuse of acronyms justifiable?' can be the moment of truth. Overuse them and acronyms become a barrier to effective communication: a stumbling block of our own creation. Far from solving a problem, they can become the problem.

For example, even assuming I have explained the acronyms I am about to use, can I ever really be justified writing the following sentence?

'The IEEE and the NCAA used the VHDL: VHSIC instead of the PHP (which had phased out the GNU).'

No, I cannot! And please do not even try to work this out; it really is as nonsensical as it looks!

Another problem can be that the same acronym can have various meanings in different contexts. For example, I have seen the following six variations listed for the acronym APAC:

Asia and Pacific;

Asia Pacific Advisory Committee;

Aboriginal Political Action Committee;

All People Are Customers;

Atlantic Pilotage Authority Canada;

Association Professionnelle des Agents Commerciaux de France (Professional Association of Commercial Agents of France).

This is not even the full list: there are more variations listed in various dictionaries. What is more, even within the same company APAC could feasibly signify 'Asia and Pacific' or 'All People Are Customers'. Confusing. It is true that, as an executive, you may have the courage to question what an acronym means if you do not know. But what about your colleagues, staff or customers? Will everyone feel confident to ask if they do not know?

As a troubleshooter called in to help companies, I readily question what unexplained acronyms mean. I am usually told 'We do not need to explain them; our target readers definitely understand these terms.' So I persist and ask them to explain the terms to me, as I definitely do not know what they mean. In very many cases, both readers (and even the writers) do not actually know. In the case of the writers, some have admitted that they did know six months previously when they wrote the acronym(s) but over time they had quite simply forgotten.

Sometimes we all have to dare to stand up and ask 'What does that mean?' or point out 'That piece of writing does not make sense.' I hope you see such objectivity as a good thing; otherwise you may be doing your readers a disservice.

Save and back up

I cannot stress enough the importance of regularly clicking the save button to save and store your writing in folders in your PC system and of keeping a copy of your writing, in case your originals get damaged. After all your hard work refining your English writing skills, you cannot run the risk of losing your business writing by accident.

Your checklist for action

- Be clear by using the right words and avoid over-complex English vocabulary.

- Use English dictionaries with care and try to coordinate with others as to which you use.

- Write with the right tone in English for your target audience; avoid seeming superior or poetic unless you definitely know this will connect with your target readers.

- Be sure that your communication makes sense – reread it critically before issuing or publishing.

- Question, if need be, to ensure that every piece of company writing in English is correct and fit for purpose.

- Use the power of clear notes in English to capture and agree outcomes of informal meetings or conversations. This is especially important in cross-cultural situations where everyone's grasp of English may not be at the same level.

- Use English acronyms in clear and unambiguous ways.

- Back up your efforts so that you do not lose your careful work in English.

7

Helping you write those documents

The mechanics of writing: how signposting will help

Signpost your ideas to yourself first, then to your readers

If, like many people, you are daunted by the thought of writing, try first to visualize an outline of what you want to say. Write down subject headings and bullet points as you think of them. Arrange them later so that they flow and your logical structure helps you shine.

Information

If something is for information tell your readers, preferably at the beginning.

Action

Action by whom? And what action? When? Why? Where? How?

If action needs to be taken, then write that down. Indicate who needs to do it. Preferably build in a timescale or actual date by which this needs to be done, and then check that it has been done.

Be sure exactly what your brief is

If you are not clear at the outset, then you cannot make good progress. Always remember that it is a sign of strength, not weakness, to ask when you are not sure, especially if you are a non-NE writer. For example, it could be that the person who has asked you to write a report is not altogether clear about this. It is a huge cost to any company not to address this problem at source.

Choose the best words for the target audience at any given time

Where possible ensure they are also words that will stay meaningful in six months, or six years or more.

Do not make things more complicated than they need be

In general, readers are more impressed when facts are presented simply. Writing simply can be more of a challenge the higher up you go in an organization. Senior executives can have a mistaken belief that complexity underlines intelligence, when the truth is that, in business writing, complexity can undermine intelligence.

Reports and executive summaries

Global companies do not always require staff to write formal reports in English. Increasingly they use presentations for status reports and proposals and so on. Or they use business reviews and collaborative reports. These are where a writer gathers facts and adds their – and others' – evaluation of these, as a business case for consideration. The review can be a question of creating an open dialogue, which may or may not lead to a conclusion in time.

Managers' collaborations

The best collaborative reports read as seamless documents. All the points made appear in a logical sequence; topics are differentiated and all recommendations are clearly argued and well thought through. This is much easier to achieve when just one person is writing a report. But executive reports often require managers to collaborate – and this is when you will find a far greater incidence of seamed reports. By this I mean reports where readers are confused by:

- noticeable differences in writing style within a report;

- obvious lack of fluidity in content and argument;

- repetition;

- lack of clear direction;

- conflicting information or recommendations.

One of the main reasons why this happens is because it is so easy to cut and paste from Word documents that others e-mail as their input to reports. But do not accept that cutting and pasting will necessarily work. One person still has to edit and make sure that the report adds up to make the correct whole – to make complete sense, in short, and to have the visible stamp of authority of that one owner.

Executive summaries

The content of every report is naturally crucial. At executive level, the considered opinion you are likely to provide should be welcome and valuable. Understanding how time-pressured your readers are likely to be, you may find an executive summary a particularly useful tool. An executive summary is just that: a summary of what the busy executive who needs to read it, needs to see. You have to hit the key messages and core data: in short, the very heart of the report instantly.

Although the summary can appear at the beginning or end of the report, many prefer it at the outset. It should briefly outline:

■ the background, current position, implications and possibilities;

■ the main findings and any changes you are recommending.

Manuals and instructions

Although you may not have to write these documents yourself, you may have to supervise those who do. Some essential points to be covered by this type of writing are summarized now.

Make sure all instructions are correctly ordered: that is, a logical sequence is followed from step one to the final step. This logical sequence has to take into account all the factors that are involved. For example, if you are itemizing the steps an electrician on a building site needs to take regarding electrical installation, do not forget that step one might not be to check that all electricity is turned off. It might be: 'Put on a safety helmet before entering the site' or 'Assemble all necessary testing equipment' and then 'Put on a safety helmet.'

As discussed in Chapter 4, there is a marked shift towards writing in the active rather than the passive voice in English. This shift is very noticeable when it comes to writing manuals and other instructions. A past preoccupation with procedures and processes is gradually giving way to the realization that it is actually people who drive procedures.

Try comparing the active construction in the next sentence with the passive construction in the sentence that follows it:

'Before you change the bulb, you must ensure that the switch is in the 'off' position.'

'Before the bulb is changed, it should be ensured that the switch is in the 'off' position.'

The first sentence makes it easier for the reader to understand that they personally must do something, and that the something is to check that the switch is in the 'off' position. The meaning in the second sentence is more oblique: maybe checking that the switch is in the 'off' position is just something that is advisable for someone (but nobody in particular) to do. Because it is less direct in style, it seems less urgent to do. Yet when we think again about the subject matter, it is surely essential that a switch is turned off before anybody changes a bulb, especially in this Health and Safety legislation-conscious age.

A similar principle applies in these further two examples. The preferred active style for manuals today is shown in the first example. The second shows the passive style:

'If you notice a problem with your appliance, please contact Customer Services.'

'Should a problem be encountered with the appliance, Customer Services may be contacted.'

Agendas, meeting notes and minutes

You may or may not have to write on these topics but you are very likely to have some role in managing the process. Why? Because the moment your minute taker records something in English, it gets recorded 'as a fact'. This can be very tricky if your minute taker is not completely proficient in English or the decision makers are not completely articulate in English.

What happens next? As a manager you get measured alongside that fact. So whatever you do, grasp the importance of checking before you leave the meeting what is going to be recorded.

Believe me, minutes are often challenged after the event when attendees hold differing perspectives. Indeed, even when everyone who attends a specific meeting is of the same nationality, they frequently challenge minutes or notes. 'Were we at the same meeting?' can be the universal complaint, as colleagues look in amazement at the record of 'decisions taken' and 'actions assigned'.

Can you imagine the extra problems there may be when different nationalities are involved? People will almost certainly have differing levels in expertise in their use of English. They are put in a position (that even a native English writer finds a real professional challenge) of having to:

■   understand what is being said in the meeting;

■   have the confidence and ability to interact in English within that meeting (which may be questioning, agreeing, debating, modifying and so on);

- make a judgement whether the decision recorded is the correct one in each case;

- ensure that all follow-up is correctly recorded and everyone knows who must do what and when they must do it by.

How you can help as a 'meetings manager'

My management career started with committee administration. I soon wondered why the written English used in reports and minutes was so very formal and stilted. During actual meetings, people spoke far more informally and far more fluidly. Being new to the organization, I did not think of questioning this. Instead I conformed and wrote in the traditional formal style.

As I grew as a manager, I realized that actually I could and should make a difference. After all, the traditional style had been new at one time. It was time for a review.

Maybe it is time for your review of the English you use in business, if you have to write agendas, notes and minutes in your company. The starting point can be for meetings managers to stop and ask themselves if there really has to be such a difference between the way people speak English and the English we use to write minutes.

It can be an unnecessary challenge for non-NE speakers to have to change from one style to another. It is true that minute takers should avoid writing slang – but why lose the voices of the people behind the decision-making process?

So do give this some thought if you are a manager who has to attend meetings, either regularly or just occasionally. If you also have to take notes (or supervise minute writing) then the following tips are likely to help you further.

Writing minutes in English is not about translating

Meetings should always happen for a purpose and the real point of meetings can actually be what gets recorded in writing.

And that record is not the end of the story. In a sense, the minutes are the beginning of the story – and the storyline is about:

- what needed to be covered;

- what was covered;

- what was closed;

- what people need to come back to.

In addition, the story has to be written in a way that can be understood by people who may not have been at the meeting. It also has to make sense six months or six years (or even longer) after the meeting took place. So it is wrong to think that writing minutes in English is just focusing on recording word for word what people said in the meeting (or the strict translation of this).

It is as much about knowing how much to write to frame those words into a meaningful background and foreground. And if extra facts are needed, then consider writing an appendix to your minutes. Make sure that this is also in English. Non-NE writers frequently revert to their own language when it comes to writing attachments, or they affix attachments that are not in English.

Highlight in the minutes that the appendix is where readers can access any additional information that some (though not all) will want and need to pick up.

Meetings and minutes can be as much about actions as anything and, even more to the point, they can be about:

- clearing actions;

- recommendations (the things that people need to go away and do);

- status (where are we up to on each action at this time?).

If you work in a global organization you will know why I am writing this. If you do not record actions in accessible English in a way that people easily see and understand who owns each action – then often nothing gets followed up, unless someone remembers it.

It can be selective amnesia; for example: 'I don't remember agreeing that!' There can even be competition between departments. That is why closing actions can be key. It can be like telling the others: 'You can see that our department delivers results.'

It will help you paint the right picture if you design a useful format to record actions and current status. That is what minutes need to do, as the summary in the box shows.

A summary table of actions

- Recently closed actions: when closed, what the outcome was.

- Open actions: plus who is responsible and any updates.

- New actions: plus who is responsible, due dates and any comments.

You can keep the table going by giving a reference code to each action with date assigned (where d = day and m = month) and sequential numbering; for example:

ddmm/01

ddmm/02

Delete older closed items as appropriate.

Converting speech into writing

How do you spell that?

If you or your staff are taking orders in English by telephone, you will probably have to write the details down for onward processing. Many companies recruit people with excellent spoken skills for these jobs, forgetting this crucial written element. After all, a sale is not a sale until the transaction is complete – and writing is so often the medium that closes the deal.

Do not be puzzled as to why I am now going to set out the NATO phonetic alphabet (also known as the international radiotelephony alphabet). It really is not only for aviation staff to learn! Businesses that write in English internationally use it to help staff spell English words that people say to them, face to face or over the telephone. Surprisingly though, it does not always feature in induction training, which is why people ask me about it.

Make use of it when you ask for confirmation that you have heard correctly, so that you can write that information down. Do not just hope for the best. That can seriously damage your business.

The alphabet is as follows:

A   Alpha

B   Bravo

C   Charlie

D   Delta

E   Echo

F   Foxtrot

G   Golf

H   Hotel

I   India

J   Juliet

K   Kilo

L   Lima

M   Mike

N   November

O   Oscar

P   Papa

Q   Quebec

R   Romeo

S   Sierra

T   Tango

U   Uniform

V   Victor

W   Whiskey

X   X-ray

Y   Yankee

Z   Zulu

Writing a date in orders

It is essential to realize that there are a number of correct ways of writing dates in UK English. The UK English format (which most of Europe uses) is:

DD / MM / YY, where D = day, M = month, Y = year.

This is in sharp contrast with the US format, which is:

MM / DD / YY.

And both are in contrast with the format used in Japan, for example, which is:

YY / MM / DD.

You can imagine the serious mistakes that can happen if a wrong assumption is made.

International date format

This has been devised to make the way we write dates internationally understandable. It is based on the following format:

YYYY – MM – DD.

In this format, YYYY refers to all the digits (eg 2015), MM refers to the month (01 to 12) and DD refers to the day (01 to 31).

When there is any doubt, it is really useful to write your dates in English this way.

Writing recruitment campaigns

I would like to cover two aspects here which depend on whether you outsource your company recruitment or recruit directly.

Oversee any outsourcing

My advice to you from the previous section naturally carries into this one: oversee any outsourcing on which you may decide. The following real-life case highlights this need. A global operator decided to outsource their campaign to recruit a supply chain manager.

The agency they chose placed an advertisement in English along the following lines:

> 'Our clients operate internationally and now seek to expand there (sic*) high quality team further. The Supply Chain Managers is (sic*) responsible for day-to-day-supplier management. This is not a learn-on-the-job role. You will be fluent in English.'

Note: *Sic is Latin for 'so' or 'thus'. Placed after a word written by someone else that we are copying or quoting, it signifies that this is how the word appears in the original version. 'Sic' is useful where you need to highlight an error, as it also distances you from that error (that is, the mistake is clearly not yours).

Returning to the text, can you see the two errors? Firstly, the writer has written 'there' for 'their'. Even if they had used the computer spellcheck, homonyms (words that sound the same but may have different meanings) can pass the check. Secondly, the position advertised is for one supply chain manager but the advertisement puts this into the plural 'Managers', while leaving the verb 'is' in the singular. So the correct grammatical possibilities are either ...

'The Supply Chain Managers are responsible for ...'

... or ...

'The Supply Chain Manager is responsible for ...'

The agreement of subject and verb (concord) rule dictates that 'The Supply Chain Managers is responsible ...' is incorrect English. You may initially feel lenient towards the writer, until you read the words: 'This is not a learn-on-the-job role. You will be fluent in English.'

The company begins to sound harsh; they are clearly implying: 'Apply for this job and you have to get it right – there is no room for learning.' But they (and/or the agency that acts for them) have not got it right. Readers can make a value judgement and might even come up with an unfavourable view about double standards. It may be a wrong judgement but the reader is more likely to think of the client company, not the agency, as being responsible.

When job descriptions can give the wrong impression

What if you do not outsource but recruit staff directly and have to write job descriptions in English? The chances are that you may well have used tired, standard expressions that you have taken from others. What you may not be aware of is this: some of these terms have become clichés. This is a loan word from French, taken into English. It means an expression that has been overused to the extent that readers are simply not impressed. (By the way, if you use a loan word in English from another language, do always check that it means what you think it means. I have found on many occasions that loan words – such as cliché – can mean different things to different nationalities. That is why I have defined its meaning here.)

So, to resume the point about clichés … if companies say the same things, year in, year out, the expressions can lose meaning or be derisible. They can make a company look like it might stifle new talent; in short, it can (inadvertently) be pushing away the people it is trying to attract.

For some light relief, let me give you some examples now. The tired, standard expressions in English are listed first; readers' possible interpretations follow:

self-motivated = nobody there to help you;

an intellectually stimulating role = this role has not yet been thought through; no chance of success (also known as a poisoned chalice: the job nobody else wants);

this position offers varied roles = you do whatever we tell you; you are a dogsbody, a gofer;

forward thinking = Help! We need ideas fast!

tact = overly sensitive workforce;

salary commensurate with experience = less than the market rate.

Outsourcing your business English writing

If you do outsource, make sure the person who briefs the agency really understands what is needed and wants to be responsible – and remains accountable throughout, right through to outcome and feedback stage. Otherwise you could face unwanted repercussions, as the airline described in the case study found out to its cost.

Case study

A major airline incurred adverse publicity and unnecessary expense when it had to rewrite its global advertising campaign. This was after it had made incorrect claims about its punctuality by referring to the high percentage of its planes that took off 'within 15 minutes of the scheduled time'.

A query was raised as to whether this measure was an industry standard – and the UK Civil Aviation Authority (CAA) were questioned about this. Their answer was that departure times were not measured at take-off but when aircraft were pushed back from the terminal. As planes routinely have to taxi before take-off, this takes time – which can be 20 minutes (depending on the airport), and longer at busy times.

Although the claim was apparently made as a result of a genuine human error, the airline had to change the wording in all its national and international advertisements.

Wherever a mix-up occurs or has occurred, the buck has to stop with the client. In this case, the client was the airline and it was ultimately accountable. Indeed this is always going to be the case when written English communication is involved. No company can ever fully outsource responsibility for that.

Your checklist for action

- Ensure the quality of reports by adopting a single style of business English writing rather than cutting and pasting.

- Include a clear summary in English for busy cross-cultural readers.

- Improve and modernize manuals and instructions in English by using the active rather than the passive voice.

- Make agendas, meeting notes and minutes a vital and cross-culturally effective management tool, by understanding how to write English that tells a continuing story.

- Remember that important verbal exchanges may only become completed business transactions when captured accurately in written English that people understand.

- Retain ownership of any outsourced communication – if it is wrong or in old-fashioned English, then it is your company's reputation that suffers.

- Avoid recycling tired English expressions (clichés).

8

Writing to lead, inspire – and change

'People' words and change

Change will feature prominently in your role as a manager and you will understand the importance of knowing how to manage it. Statistics show us that so many change initiatives fail, not least because they can cause ripples of uncertainty. Staff can feel anxious, even threatened. Managers too can feel 'Things were fine just the way they were' (the implication being: 'My leadership was working').

It is true that no company has to change – but it is also true that companies that do not change may not survive. Business English writing can either help or hinder in driving these changes forward. Get it right and there is virtually no cost involved, only the benefits of getting your people on side. Get it wrong and many of your initiatives may die.

So how do you lead people through the medium of your English writing? Involve staff in the changes. Encourage everyone to develop strong working relationships. Lead by example.

A word of warning here: although broader business change presents an opportunity to change a company's communication style, it is best not to be too radical. It can work against you to go overnight from style A to style B, as demonstrated in the extracts in the box.

Communicating change: style A

Because of the changes being implemented throughout the company, driven by an identified need to change the existing business model, it is essential that staff acquaint themselves with the new company values and that these are followed strictly at all times.

Communicating change: style B

Let's welcome this great new start and embrace change whole-heartedly. Let's see work as fun and enjoy growing the company and improving greater profitability for all stakeholders. Get up to speed with our new values and get on board today!

Not only may such a radical contrast in the two styles confuse staff, it may irritate their cultural sensibilities. They may feel even like the 'new outsiders' because they cannot easily relate to the new style. It can compound their resistance to change.

In such instances, it can be very useful and productive for you to identify a transitional style. It introduces a new start but is inclusive at the same time, such as style C in the next box.

> **Communicating change: style C**
>
> We are all beginning a new journey together. We have a clear vision to take us all forward to new opportunities and growth and will seize the opportunity to work with all staff to draw up new values that we can all relate to, as we proceed down this new path to success.

Many companies find that an inclusive style works really well in cross-cultural settings. It has the effect of making staff generally feel valued and understand that change can indeed be for the better. What is more, the style has a levelling effect: 'We are all in this together, so let's get on, work together and enjoy sharing the rewards.'

The 'What's in it for me?' factor

Change is not only about company change; it can also be about the change made by an individual's personal self-development. Indeed, every time I design a training programme, I design it to make a measurable difference not only to attendees' personal performance but also to overall company success. I end each course with a request to delegates:

- Please record now, in writing, three things that you will do differently (and better) as a direct result of this course.

- Please continue to identify what you see as best writing practice around you.

- Share this best practice with your teams.

This highly specific, highly targeted practice can pay far higher dividends than any evaluation sheet. It focuses solely on the individual and what this course means to them and covers the 'What's in it for me?' factor. Interestingly, the moment we set down our views in writing, it seems we are more likely to act on our findings. That is what I see from my attendees' tangible and sustainable improvements, even after attending just one workshop.

Jargon, including management speak and legalese

Jargon generally

Jargon can be defined as words or expressions used by a particular profession or group that are difficult (sometimes unnecessarily difficult) for others to understand. As a consultant, I naturally deal with a great many companies and am confident enough to query what their jargon means. Sometimes they cannot explain, being baffled by their own words. It is yet another salutary lesson and if you can avoid jargon, do so!

Examples of English jargon often used in the public sector are:

partnership working (= working together);

holistic governance (= overall management);

community empowerment (= encouraging the public to do things for themselves);

bottom up (= listening to people).

Management speak and buzzwords

Management speak and buzzwords are a specific type of jargon used by executives all over the world. Just as in the public sector examples, they inflate simple expressions into something that they (mistakenly) think sounds more impressive. Examples are:

blue-sky thinking;

joined-up thinking;

singing from the same hymn sheet;

movers and shakers;

push (or stretch) the envelope;

360-degree thinking;

this is on my radar;

it needs to be incentivized.

I am deliberately not going to explain what all these expressions mean, or what I think they mean, which may be different. In fact, it would be hard to get any group of NE speakers to agree.

So imagine what may happen when different nationalities are involved. What will their individual understanding be? Put them together in a group and you may not get the outcome the management speaker expects. So if 'picking the low hanging fruit' means going for the easy solution, the quick win, why not write or say that outright?

Even expressions you may consider common currency, such as 'the bottom line is ...' can really irritate readers. This is usually on two counts. Non-users often find the expressions pretentious and also sense that they are used in an elitist way to suggest: 'We managers have our own language. Be one of us by using and understanding (or pretending to understand) these words and expressions.' Interestingly, 'text-speak' is often having a parallel effect of polarizing users and non-users, as we will see later in the book.

Legalese

This is the term specifically given to jargon used by the legal profession or people writing on matters with legal implications. Of course, when you write English for legal matters, you have to get every detail and every word right in all your contractual documents.

What you also need to be aware of is this: where you need to explain matters to your layman customers (that is, those who are not members of the legal profession), use plain English. Interestingly enough, even in the UK, native readers complain about legalese: they have neither the time nor the inclination to try to work out what their lawyers mean, nor do they want to be patronized.

As a consumer, do be alert to the fact that you need to read legalese very carefully indeed. It is very easy to fall prey to scams, as global fraudsters often falsely imitate English legal writing, specifically to deceive unsuspecting international readers. Luckily for him, a Dutch friend of mine recently asked me to look over a 'contract of employment' that was written in English for a job overseas. This had been forwarded to him by e-mail.

The document looked genuine to him – but at a glance I could see that the English was over-embellished, legalese gobbledegook. A native English reader could see that something was not quite right. In fact, the document was part of a scam to obtain passports fraudulently.

My friend, however, suspected nothing untoward; the wording seemed exactly as he would expect in a legal document, written in a subset of English vocabulary he did not expect fully to understand.

A word of warning: if things do not appear to be genuine, they generally are not. When in doubt, ask for expert advice. Here is an example of legalese in English writing:

> 'For the purposes of calculating your maximum benefits under these regulations (which supersede the regulations previously in force) it could be that it would be advantageous, as it appears that you are so affected thereby, to elect that the regime will apply to you. Persons who do not make any such election remain under the purview of the previous regime of benefits which remain applicable to them.'

What does this mean? If you understood it easily you will have been one of the few who did. Can you see how writing it in plain English is going to make its meaning more accessible? The gist becomes:

> 'So that we can calculate your maximum benefits under these current regulations, please confirm if you wish to enter the scheme (which we think may benefit you). If we do not hear from you, your existing benefits still apply.'

The writer now appears to be a person, not an automaton. They seem to have the reader's interests more in mind, even though the subject matter is identical. The writing achieves this by focusing on using 'people' words and the active voice, and eliminating the details that necessarily appear in the appropriate regulations – but that only the administrators of the scheme need to know in depth.

'Everyone is equal' versus hierarchical systems

When you write English for business, it helps to understand that some cultures build formality into their languages and observe hierarchical protocol; others believe in informality and equality at all times. One illustration of this lies in the distinctions some languages have between a familiar form of 'you' in the singular person, and a formal version of 'you' in the singular person (which does not exist in English).

In German, as an example, this distinction manifests as the informal '*du*' and the formal '*Sie*' respectively. An additional formality in the language is in areas such as how to address people. If you write not just to a medical doctor – but even to a certain level of graduate – in Germany, they will expect to be addressed either as '*Herr Doktor*' (masculine) or '*Frau Doktor*' (feminine). It simply does not work in English, though. If we translate them into the English ''Mr Doctor' or 'Mrs Doctor', this is simply not a construction that sounds or looks right.

English grammar can therefore act as a leveller in language, and the language used today tends to be informal rather than formal, as you have seen throughout this book. 'You' is a word that refers to everyone, regardless of position or status within an organization.

Use the right words to motivate

Even native English writers can be surprised at the negative reactions their words can stir up. This can be totally unintentional; they may think their writing is entirely suitable for purpose. To avoid provoking such actions, it can be very helpful to categorize (in the broadest terms) the sort of words you are likely to use when writing English for business:

Positive words (that readers generally prefer)

- please
- thank you
- well done
- congratulations
- thanks for your support / all your efforts / hard work
- I value your input
- very; most

Negative words (that readers may prefer not to see):

- no
- can't/cannot
- impossible
- failure
- quite
- words that imply I versus you, us versus them

Relationship-building phrases (that many readers will prefer):

- it would greatly assist me/us if you could …
- I know that it's year end and you are very busy, but may I just ask …
- how is it going?
- phrases that imply me and you, us and them

Any list you compile is likely to be of practical assistance to you. For example, you have to get some information and you have to get it quickly. That is when you can use the words that are likely to help you – and avoid words that are likely to hinder you.

As an example, have you ever wondered why people write 'Please bear with me, I am not good at this' or 'I am sorry if this is not very well prepared'? They can actually make their readers think 'This writing is going to be rubbish.'

Of course there are times when you have to write negative English in order to achieve your objectives. If a working environment is hazardous, there are things employees must not do. They must not enter or work on the site without a safety helmet, for example. So you can write: 'Do not enter or work on this site without wearing a safety helmet.'

You could also write: 'Danger: you must wear a safety helmet on this site at all times.'

In the second version there is a reason why the helmet must be worn (danger) and negative has been made to sound more positive, yet just as essential as before.

I am surprised how many people from diverse companies throughout the world admit that they have a reputation as the office 'Rottweiler' (a fierce dog) in the way they 'bark' orders at their colleagues. To a person, they are the most conscientious and results-driven workers and often highly friendly in face-to-face communication. Why then does something happen when they set their questions, or requirements, in business English writing?

It is normally because their writing is overly task-driven and heavy-handed in approach. It lacks the personal touch that can make all the difference between success and failure.

So what is most interesting is that, by changing the way they wrote English, using the tips I have just given, these formerly harsh writers found that:

- they generally got more assistance;

- they achieved better outcomes;

- even though nothing about their personalities had changed, they found they were still viewed in a far more favourable light.

Writing English to lead and motivate just got easier!

Burying good news

When large organizations have to release bad news (such as a major downturn in profits or large-scale redundancies) they often choose days when they know media attention is on a major international story. Their bad news will get less publicity. The practice has become known as 'burying bad news'. This is understandable enough; what is less well understood is the practice of burying good news.

If you bury good news in business, you basically hide positive messages or great results and, by implication, fail to motivate or delight others. It can happen when managers get preoccupied with writing that fits preset and categorized headings – and fail to think of the real message they need to communicate.

This can be linked to the false belief that business writing is about ticking checklists of things to cover, or even points to translate into English. I have highlighted both phenomena earlier in this book.

The next example illustrates how one manager inadvertently got it wrong (at least from her team's point of view), despite the fact that her intentions were good. Read the next box and see what happened.

Issues and concerns

It was a matter of great concern whether the team would be able to function during this manager's maternity break, particularly as orders were up 15 per cent on the same period last year.

There were contingency plans in action in case the team found themselves unable to deliver but, in the event and contrary to expectations, they managed to complete on time and within budget.

If we analyse this extract from the beginning, we can see that the topic heading 'Issues and concerns' sounds very negative from the outset. The writer has set the scene; readers almost expect bad news to follow. Yet what actually is the key message here? Is it negative? Far from it: we find that the division is prospering (orders were up 15 per cent on the same period last year) and the team absolutely delivered on time and within budget, even though their manager (the writer) was on maternity break.

If we are to write to motivate and inspire, we need to understand that we ditch headings that unnecessarily fill us with doom and gloom. If our teams are doing well (particularly in the face of adverse conditions), then be proud of them – and express congratulations.

Instead of the heading 'Issues and concerns', the writer could (and should) have used a heading such as 'Congratulations to all staff for excellent results'.

The extract in the next box is very similar and demonstrates how widespread the practice of burying good news is.

However, despite the continuing decline in the manufacturing sector generally, our company appeared to outperform the overall market in October.

To fill you in on the background, the company in question had indeed outperformed the market – against the prevailing trend in the manufacturing sector. The verb 'appeared' (which means 'seemed') was inappropriate here and has the effect of diluting the good news. The very first word 'However' sets an unjustifiably negative scene. Once again, the manager in question would have motivated and inspired colleagues by expressing congratulations to all staff for their great achievements in clearly difficult times.

Your checklist for action

- Take care when changing communication style in English – consider a transitional style when this is part of a broader business change.

- Use jargon and management speak sparingly and only when really appropriate in written English communication.

- Explain legalese in plain English wherever possible.

- Remember that formality and hierarchy are often not present in English grammar and spelling.

- Do not lose sight of the fact that it is people who drive processes, and they relate positively to 'people' words.

- Do not bury good news in writing and avoid English words and phrases that demotivate.

- Instead write English positively to express good news where you can, and see how it can have a positive effect on your business performance.

- Words that are unnecessarily negative or divisive are not going to build key, sustainable, or indeed any, relationships!

- If you really must write negative news, always explain, sensitively, the reasons why you must do so.

9

Writing e-mails

Setting standards: corporate policy

It undoubtedly makes a great deal of commercial sense for companies to have a policy regarding e-mails and text messages. They often use a checklist of questions that are likely to help, such as:

- Is e-mail our preferred mode of corporate communication or corporate writing?

- Otherwise, when should staff write e-mail?

- Do we have a corporate style, format, font, point size?

- Do we use UK or US English spelling, or a variant?

- Are there subjects that are off-limits in e-mail?

- Do we instruct all staff on how to write English for business?

■ Are staff encouraged to ask for help when they are not sure?

■ Do we foster a positive culture and a supportive environment?

■ What do we do when we see that people are making mistakes when writing English for business?

■ Are managers willing to help?

■ Do we have an induction handbook that sets out these points?

Monitoring policy

If you decide to implement a policy you do, of course, need to monitor it and update it regularly. This is especially important as new channels for writing on the internet are opening all the time. Facebook, MySpace, Linked In are established as I write, but new sites are continuously appearing and staff may be using these in work time.

Employers may not be aware that they can be held vicariously responsible in law for the acts of employees who access these sites at work. If any comments that staff post are found to be libellous, then employers may face financial consequences should damages be awarded to the person or company against whom the defamatory writing is directed. Naturally this also applies if any senior employee of a company were to write or authorize defamatory writing about a competitor.

Subjects that staff should know are off-limits in e-mail and text messages

As a manager, you need to know (and ensure that that your staff know) that certain topics should not be covered in e-mails. Drawing up a general policy can help make both existing and new staff aware that they must not write e-mails or text messages that:

■   refer to age, disability, sexual, racial, religious or ethnic topics which may be considered to be discriminatory in nature;

■   refer to anything that could potentially be classed as libel, or otherwise lead to legal action;

■   deliver bad news.

This is a starting point; you will have other topics to include in your organization.

How e-mails can impede performance

Passing e-mails on: avoiding the 'black hole of inaction'

Many companies are noticing how injudicious use of e-mails can lead to new problems in the workplace. In the past, staff perhaps more easily understood what problems were theirs to solve. Any associated paperwork was clearly visible in a pending tray on their desk, until sorted and filed. However, when staff receive e-mails that set out problems, it is just so easy to forward this to someone else and assume they will then deal with it, without ever actually checking that they do.

This is what I mean by e-mails leading to a 'black hole of inaction'. When we exchange details of a problem by passing an e-mail on, we may lose sight of that problem, whether intentionally or not. It all too often means that the problem remains not only unsolved, but effectively lost in the ether. This is business inefficiency in the extreme. Avoid using e-mails to pass over your responsibility for dealing with issues and completing all necessary actions.

Even if you press 'delete', e-mails can come back to haunt you

In e-mail's infancy, writers tended to see it as transitory casual conversation that required speed of response. They wrote something, pressed the 'send' button, then pressed 'delete' to empty the folder and that was the job done, until the next time. Today's writers know that this is simplistic. Even if you think you have deleted things at your end, receivers may be printing your e-mails and using them as evidence (even against you). People have lost jobs over this and cases have gone to litigation.

What are the common traps that can trip you up when you write e-mails, even despite your best intentions? The following crop up regularly:

■ Speed can lead you into mistakes in meaning or spelling or grammar, especially if English is not your first language.

■ Reacting too quickly may mean you do not write a fully considered reply and there may be far-reaching consequences that you should have anticipated.

■ Replying in the heat of the moment may mean you write things you regret.

■ Failing to understand that e-mail is not conversation (though it may seem that way) can mean you use English idiom, nuances and irony that are not appropriate for e-mails (as your reader cannot check what you mean and may misunderstand or even be offended).

Write it only if you are prepared to (and can) say it

I have heard it suggested that the computer screen of everyone who writes e-mails for business should have a sign at the top, saying 'Don't send it without thinking about it first. And don't write anything that you would not feel able to say to its reader.'

I would like to add something else as well: do not write it if you cannot pronounce it. Writers sometimes trap themselves by choosing a word that they cannot pronounce. The trouble is, they may have to read it out loud at a future date, for example in a presentation.

A practical example

Let's say you are a non-NE writer who works in human resources. It is often the case that you may find it difficult to pronounce the word 'human'. Saying 'HR' might be easier for you, unless it is simply the letter 'h' that is hard for you to pronounce.

Then you might be better off describing which area you work in: learning and development, pensions and so on; maybe even personnel in general. There are always solutions: the English language will always be able to provide you with alternative words that you will be able to pronounce, so write those instead.

Tone and etiquette

Time and time again, people complain about how annoyed they are by poor tone (and lack of manners generally) in business writing today, most specifically in e-mails. On the one hand, some readers view some e-mail messages as overly casual in style, where writers regard e-mail as conversation. On the other hand, other writers' messages can be interpreted as cold and impersonal if they have cut out words that would convey conversational tone. It is quite a challenge, therefore, to convey the right tone for all your readers at any given time.

Practical examples

Compare and contrast the tone in these extracts from real-life e-mails:

'Why haven't you done what I asked you yesterday?' (overly direct)

'Thanks loads ☺' (overly casual)

'Therefore, although it is imperative that some assessment is made, it would appear that this is probably not the right channel in which to raise the matter at the current time but it might be advantageous to seek a more opportune moment in the not too distant future.' (overly formal)

Can you think of better ways to write each example in English, to get the tone right for e-mail? Tips to help you get the tone right generally are these. Before you press 'send' on your e-mail draft, check the following:

- Is this e-mail written professionally and correctly for purpose (neither too casual nor too formal)?

- Is my e-mail polite and does it convey a virtual handshake, to pull the reader towards me and my company – rather than push them away?

- If I know my recipient's preferred style, am I mirroring that as far as possible?

- Have I invited comments from my reader periodically, to check they understand and will respond the way I expect?

Text messages: not always appropriate

The amazingly fast-growing use of text messaging (or texting or text-speak, as it is also known) demonstrates how easy and popular this form of communication is. Yet the usefulness of texting as corporate communication is something that companies need to question, and whether they need to issue staff guidelines on this. This is because professional writing is not just about easiness; we also have to think about the appropriateness of the medium we choose at any given time, how effective it is in transmitting business messages accurately and whether it will positively contribute to our brand image.

It is a known fact that where guidelines are not set, businesses can find text abbreviations becoming assimilated into their previously more formal business writing. Readers, though, do not always like it. The day may come when this practice is widely accepted; but judging from my clients' highly vocal feedback, that day is not here yet.

I have already mentioned how very many readers react negatively to overly casual e-mails, so it is highly unlikely that the same readers are suddenly going to welcome text expressions as valid business communication. Those who do not object on grounds of informality may still have a problem when it comes to meaning.

Let's take the example of 'LOL'. This can mean 'laugh out loud' or 'lots of love'. So it is tricky, to say the least, to use this in an office situation. Then again, if you use predictive text, this can complete words wrongly (even when used by NE writers) – which can again have negative (even if unintended) repercussions.

Let's take another real-life example of a text message in a business context: 'con.call.tom.'

What does this mean? It is not immediately apparent. If there is someone called Tom in your organization, it may look like 'Con, call Tom.'

The writer actually meant it as shorthand for 'There will be a conference call tomorrow' but the NE recipient was confused as to what it meant. The abbreviations were not as they would have expected. Naturally enough, a non-NE receiver is likely to be even more puzzled, which means the message becomes counter-productive.

The criticisms many people currently make of text messages tend to fall into these categories:

- What do the English text abbreviations mean?

- Text-speak can create barriers just as other jargon does. It can be another way of implying (even if unintentionally) 'If you don't understand this, you're not in my club.'

- Text-speak (particularly when assimilated into other writing modes) may demonstrate a slackening in quality and professionalism: anything goes.

The politics of address lists

When you need to send an e-mail to a list of people in your cross-cultural organization, do you ever work out the order in which to list their names? If you do, do you list names in alphabetical order? At one time I would have thought this made a great deal of sense. Now I qualify this by suggesting that it makes sense where people are of the same grade within an organization.

Why have I changed my mind about using alphabetical lists as the norm? It is because feedback constantly suggests that most recipients do notice where their names appear in any list. Different cultures can vary on this one. Some actively look for their name; some may only notice on a less conscious level.

A predominant finding is that the higher the rank in the company, the more an executive expects their name to be among the first to appear in any list. If this does not happen, I have heard them grumble about it to others, sometimes half-jokingly – but it clearly bothers them. For others, their reactions can be more extreme and they actually take offence. Yet the writers may never know this. All they see is that their English communication is straightforward and correct. They mistakenly feel that what they have done cannot possibly be misunderstood.

My tip here is take a different view and be one step ahead. The difference between success and failure can be simply to stop, think and anticipate. If you do need to send lists within your organization, see whether the following checklist may help you and your staff.

When sending an e-mail to a list of main recipients:

- Ensure the names on the list start with internal readers.

- The chief executive had better be first!

- Then work your way down the pecking order of seniority and list names in that order.

- If people are of the same grade, then you can list them alphabetically.

- Now list your external readers, using the same rule.

- Reread the order of names and check it is right.

- Send.

Sending information by e-mail to key people

Of course, every single person is highly valuable within every company. I am only making a distinction here about key people because, in practice, the more senior people in any global company can have even more demanding expectations. It is essential that writers do not waste their time. So this advice is given purely on that basis.

If you have to send, say, a report by e-mail to a key person, you could consider using a formula to help. For example:

- You could provide a very short summary in English.

- You could highlight key points (maybe by numbering or in bullet points or in colour – though preferably not red and green, as quite a number of people are colour-blind in relation to these two colours).

- Anticipate likely questions in accessible English, so that the reader does not waste time having to ask them, and set out your answers in advance.

The example in the box illustrates this approach.

Subject: ABC Report – for which your approval (in part) is needed

I attach this report, which covers the following topics:

1. Current status of ABC project.

2. Unexpected contingencies.

3. Staffing implications.

You will see that your approval is requested on the recommendations made with regard to 2 and 3, so that we can submit this to the board next Tuesday, 15 May.

Please can you review and confirm that the contingency position suggested is adequate for your area of the project and that the proposed extra staffing is appropriate and likely to be available (with the required expertise) in the time period required?

I would also be grateful if you could let me have any other observations you have on the status of the project and the paper in general.

Because I need to get the paper out to the board, please may I have your input by 5pm on Thursday, 10 May at the latest, and preferably before?

Many thanks.

John Smith

This approach is also particularly valuable when sending out agendas and papers for key meetings where you know particular items may be contentious or complex. These items can be particularly tricky for delegates who are not completely proficient in English.

Use a covering e-mail to draw attention to those items and request that attendees take note and prepare beforehand. If you know that the information sent will necessitate further discussion, you could indicate that by writing something along the following lines at the end:

'It would be good if we could explore this further.'

Taking all these factors into account, if all the information you have set out is correct, you are likely to be noticed by these key people for all the right reasons, including:

- for being systematic;

- for thinking around the subject;

- for making their life easier, whether they are NE speakers or not.

It clearly makes your life easier too when you get your e-mail right first time. Even if your recipient raises unforeseen questions, at least you will have avoided the obvious ones!

Prioritizing urgency

Even if you do not think that what you are writing about needs a strict deadline, it still streamlines performance if you indicate when the information or action is needed. You can express this in different ways; for example: 'The deadline for this is by COB tomorrow, 12 November.' (Note: I have used the abbreviation COB deliberately, which I mentioned in Chapter 1 as an abbreviation for 'close of business'. Many non-NE readers will not recognise it. Do be careful when you use acronyms when writing English across cultures.)

If the action has a lower priority, you could write something along the lines of: 'Next week will be fine.'

There is absolutely no point in any executive prioritizing the wrong things. When you must expend that energy, expend it efficiently.

Mistakes in others' e-mails

As I have mentioned, e-mails can be viewed as writing that falls halfway between formal writing and conversation. This can make people ask for company guidance on what to do about mistakes they frequently see in the e-mails they are sent. Naturally enough, this can be particularly problematic where NE speakers are being sent e-mails with mistakes by their foreign counterparts. Is it wrong to undermine non-NE writers' confidence, when they are making great efforts to communicate in another language? Or is it better to correct their mistakes in a positive, supportive way?

Let me give some examples. In English, the word 'training' exists in the singular but not in the plural. Even if we are talking about 20 courses, we simply refer to these as 'training', not 'trainings'. Similarly, we use the word 'information' in the singular, so we would never write 'Tourist informations'. Yet quite routinely non-NE writers write these non-existent plurals.

This is another area that you may think needs some guidelines – because although readers will understand the meaning of 'trainings' etc, how will writers know that this is not standard English, if they are not told? And if you then agree that it is helpful to point these things out, how do you do this tactfully?

My advice is this:

■ Make sure that there is a culture where it is definitely known that it is a strength to ask.

■   See this through – because, human nature being what it is, some staff will put questions to their line managers only to be greeted by obvious annoyance at 'being bothered'.

■   Offer support if your staff are routinely getting things wrong.

E-mail writing skills in spoken skills environments

It is essential to stress that most of us have to write in business today. It is no longer just about appointing people with great spoken communication skills, even in environments where, traditionally, spoken skills prevailed. Two very obvious areas that we all see as users are doctors' or dentists' surgeries, where receptionists now generally have to be computer and e-mail literate.

Sales or customer service contact centres are major examples of two such environments in business. Just about all of us are customers who, at one point or another, need to call a contact centre. You say what you need to say – and you hope that the adviser deals with this politely and efficiently, and speaks to you in the way you expect. Now think about what is likely to happen after you conclude the call. The spoken part of the transaction is just part of the story.

Once again, writing in English features largely in any follow-up. Why? Companies that trade globally find that their daily call logs record a high incidence of advisers having to write follow-up e-mails in English. They pass these to others inside and maybe outside the organization. These then have to be processed, in order that the next phase in the transaction (or whatever is under discussion) can proceed.

It calls for good English writing skills to ensure that this follow-up is efficient and that the correct message is:

- captured correctly and efficiently;

- relayed fast and effectively;

- correctly acted on by the recipient.

Every company benefits from streamlining performance in this way. It really reduces costs, at the same time enhancing staff skills and demonstrably improving service to valuable customers. Getting it right also shows customers that they are valued – and this is surely a major driver of overall business success.

Your checklist for action

- Set corporate standards and policy for use of e-mails as business communication in English both internally and to external parties.

- Be clear who needs to respond or act, and avoid injudicious forwarding of e-mail chains.

- Always consider carefully what you have written before sending.

- Consider tone and address-list etiquette for your cross-cultural audience.

- Only allow English text-speak when your audience is ready – the time may come, but it is not yet universally acceptable.

- Use covering e-mails in English to good effect, and as an effective cross-cultural management tool when circulating papers electronically – to gain the right outcomes and get noticed for the right reasons.

■ Emphasize the importance of effective written English for e-mail communication in international customer services, contact and call centre environments.

10

Feedback and performance reviews

How to give feedback in English

Just about every manager has to give feedback at some stage. Because of the nature of appraisals in business today, this almost always involves filling in an appraisal form.

Some people dread having to do this even in their own language, so it can be quite a daunting task to have to write in English for cross-cultural appraisals – and send a copy to each employee in advance, for their comments. They then have to write these in English too.

Case study

A native English-speaking senior manager of a global multinational company experienced unexpected problems when writing and receiving feedback on and from his cross-cultural teams.

Although clearly expert in using English that would be understood by NE speakers, he realized that some non-native English-speaking staff did not understand his evaluations. What was more, he did not understand some of their feedback either.

Together we identified the problem. It was that the lack of a common parlance was causing outright confusion. Like was not being compared with like. That is never good in business. In view of this, I devised a glossary of English terms for feedback ratings, which you will find set out later in this chapter.

And what was the manager's verdict? This is worth its weight in gold. He was able to eradicate the wide variation in writing and meanings that had caused the problems. And he spread the message throughout the company, wishing that this diagnostic writing tool had been identified years ago.

When 'fair' might equal 'bad'

When giving feedback in writing, non-NE speakers often write perfectly constructed sentences – but the English words they choose don't always give the full and accurate meaning of their thoughts.

For example, they may write that somebody has made a 'good effort' where a native English speaker may write 'excellent effort'. This difference may, at first sight, seem minimal.

But there can be an unexpected and unwanted knock-on effect where people's efforts or achievements are understated – just because an evaluator chose the wrong English word.

Your staff can feel bad about it. And understandably, it can affect performance.

When 'quite' might equal 'very'

Even UK and US English can vary significantly. I remember one American head teacher referring to the fact that he was 'quite proud' of a pupil's outstanding academic achievement.

To a native English reader this qualification 'quite' can dilute the degree of pride. The expression then appears to mean 'slightly proud' – although I have no doubt the teacher was very proud indeed of his star pupil.

'On the right track'; or have you reached your destination?

A non-native English senior manager once wrote in an appraisal of a first-class management trainee (who was a native English speaker) that the employee was 'on the right track'.

Their intended meaning was 'This employee is doing well.' But the meaning understood by the native reader was 'This employee is not yet where he needs to be.'

The bright young trainee felt aggrieved that his boss had written in his performance review that he was only 'on the right track'. He felt that he was much further on than being 'on track'. In his opinion, he had just about reached his destination – and was ready for promotion.

Ironically, his boss agreed – but his English had not expressed this. His writing had unintentionally alienated the person he had meant to support.

Lose (or quit) your job because of the wrong English word?

Let's discuss this point further. What if job cuts are to be made? All things being equal, who goes first? Should it be the people who have arrived at their destination, ie who are where they want to be, at the top and performing strongly, as the company wants them to do?

Or are the people more likely to be 'let go' (made redundant) those who are straggling, even struggling to 'get there' and, by inference, to achieve their goals?

As a senior executive using English, you will understand the significance of what I am saying. But you have probably never seen it in a self-help book on English before. It is about time it was – because imagine losing your job just because your boss used the wrong English word! Or imagine feeling like quitting because of that same wrong choice of English word. Use of English impacts on performance and results.

In the box is another real-life example to show you the importance of getting your English right.

Case study

In the sales and marketing division of one international business association, an employee who excelled at her job unexpectedly quit, giving the minimum of notice.

Why? She knew she was great at her job and expected highly positive feedback when her boss was reviewing her performance in sales and customer service. She knew that she was better than 'good' and would have been seriously offended by being rated as 'quite good'.

But what her boss did was even worse than this – to her way of thinking at least. Even though he knew she was a first-class member of staff, he did not express this to her. Instead he wrote 'satisfactory' for her rating in these two areas of performance. It is a correct English word – but it was exactly the wrong word in this context.

She was incensed when she read the rating. Rather than argue her case, she decided that enough was enough. She sought and secured a job elsewhere, within weeks. The company lost a star employee for entirely the wrong reasons.

What is almost worse is that that particular boss has not learnt he should change his approach and choice of written English. So a similar occurrence is likely to happen again in that company.

Can your company afford to risk the kind of occurrence described? It shows how different nationalities may overstate or understate things. It can help cross-cultural readers to know the nationality of the writer. Native English speakers might look for subtle nuances and clues from fellow native speakers, and understand how to read between the lines. But when readers know that non-NE writers are involved, they will not expect the same clues and are likely to make different allowances. It is important for your business to understand this.

Problems need not arise if you evaluate the right English for your audience. For example, consider whether you have come across terms that irritated or confused you. If so, write down as many as you can think of in the box below, and learn to avoid them. Check with colleagues to see if they feel the same way about them.

Feedback terms that irritate or confuse

Feedback ratings: other differences

General

Ratings go from 0 to 5, where 0 = poor and 5 = excellent:

0 = poor, unsatisfactory

1 = adequate, satisfactory

2 = quite good, room for improvement, reasonably good attempt

3 = good

4 = very good

5 = great, excellent, outstanding, first class, role model

Even within a single culture (take the UK as an example) there will be a split between people who:

- are comfortable with describing first-class performance using the words I attribute to the top rating, 5;

- are uncomfortable with so doing, and will use the words I attribute to the second-to-top rating, 4;

- feel that 'room for improvement' must apply to all levels (because we cannot ever reach perfection).

Improvement ratings

This is another area where ratings expressed in English might help you.

The ratings go from 0 to 5, where 0 = not improving and 5 = improving strongly:

0 = not improving, no improvement

1 = not improving adequately, no satisfactory improvement, no discernible improvement

2 = slight improvement

3 = improving adequately, satisfactory improvement

4 = improving well, good improvement, marked improvement

5 = improving strongly, strong improvement, impressive improvement, outstanding improvement

Star ratings

Here is another example of how ratings in English can confuse when interpreted differently by different readers. Each year the UK Audit Commission assesses the performance of UK local authorities and the services they provide for local people. This is called the Comprehensive Performance Assessment (CPA), against which a local council or other public service is given a rating.

Now bear in mind that the ratings are all about seeing services from the public's perspective. Thus the ratings have to be expressed in a way that the public can easily relate to. The Commission decided that the following ratings would fit the bill nicely:

4 stars (excellent)

3 stars (good)

2 stars (fair)

1 star (weak)

0 stars (poor)

This is the system that has been operating for a number of years now and councils that achieve the 4-star rating are delighted to do so. But some members of the public (their target audience) are less proud of them than you might think. Do you know why?

It is because a 0- to 4-star rating makes many of the target audience think of hotel ratings, where 5 stars (or, as I write, the bar is being raised to 6 or 7 stars) are the badge of excellence. And whenever we write English in business, we must keep in mind why we are writing and who our readers are. So in this instance, target readers' expectations might well be that, for their councils to be excellent, they need to achieve a 5-star rating.

Can you imagine how all these issues can become even more complicated when differing cultures are involved? Every time we write, we need to see things from our readers' perspective and make sure that the system we use is as foolproof as possible. Put simply: are our words in English really saying what we mean them to say to our readers?

Your checklist for action

■ Be aware that some words may have different nuances for native English and non-native English readers: this may have unintended effects in the sensitive area of cross-cultural staff appraisal.

■ Design a glossary of ratings terms in English for each scenario where these are needed.

■ Use this as common parlance in business English – to reduce misunderstandings and avoid causing unintentional offence.

Conclusion

With all that you have learnt in this book, you are in the forefront of business writing today. You are now in the new generation of Word Power Skills 2.0 – understanding how to make your total written communication in English cohesive and customer centred.

You will feel confident and knowledgeable – not only about writing totally professional business English yourself but about knowing how to supervise your teams to do the same.

So many managers look at the most expensive solutions to their business communication problems. Yet, as this book shows, the practical advice I give about bringing word power skills to your English business writing is a virtually free resource. You have absolutely nothing to lose and so much to gain by using this invaluable tool kit in order to write great English for today's business.

Here is a guideline to help you plan what you actively intend to work on:

■ This can be on a personal level.

■ It can also be on a corporate level. Have you identified any initiatives that are needed? If so, what are they? Who will champion them – and how?

■ Have you identified best practice? How will you share this with your colleagues and teams?

■ Anything else?

Once again we have a manifestation of written word power. Once you write an idea down, it is more likely to become reality. Did you know that? So take the opportunity of writing down the topics you are going to work on – and who you are going to involve.

The written word acts as clothes to our logic. Enjoy harnessing its power, to take you and your business forward, both easily and successfully.

I will end the book with this essential and empowering observation:

crucial to success is always to remember: great communication does not just happen; we have to design it to work.

The Preface to this book explains how the series fits together, to offer you a comprehensive and invaluable reference guide for almost all aspects of your writing English for business needs.